# Noun Hear This!

## A Companion Handbook for
## Students of German

C.S. Stahlman

# DEDICATION

To all students of German who not only think about the language but also feel an admiration and affection for it that only speakers of it experience

# ACKNOWLEDGMENTS

Thank you to Frau Schlicksbier, my high school teacher who arranged the exchange student opportunity where I also met the woman who would become my wife and my son's mother.

I am thankful for my father, who taught me the poem "Der gute Kamerad," and for his father, who prayed Psalm 145:15 in German at mealtimes during my childhood.

I am forever grateful to Julia Ward as Editor-in-Chief and coach who cheerfully shouldered the details of commas, fonts, organization, and similar things that burden me.

I also thank the University of Illinois Department of Germanic Languages and Literature—particularly Dr. Zachary Hader, who led the technical review with hours of contribution; Dr. Charles Webster, the Director of the Basic Language Program; and Dr. Walker Horsfall, whose direction led me to Dr. Webster and Dr. Hader.

Also most helpful was Ingrid Ippach of Southeast High School in Springfield, IL, who came through with much-needed technical feedback and encouragement along with pedagogical insights. Impressively, she also teaches Spanish at the high school.

Thanks also to Fiverr and to Kathy Carpenter, who designed the eye-catching book cover.

I remain grateful to my son, whom I love and who often teaches me things I've not considered. Gratitude also goes to my mom (who, along with my father, often wondered about my enjoyment of languages but let me go my own route anyway) and to my sister (a refreshing gust of wind in my sails as I pursued collecting nouns and going through the publication process).

# CONTENTS

# PART I:

# UNDERSTANDING GERMAN NOUNS

# 1

# INTRODUCTION

Welcome to *Noun Hear This!* "Deutsche Sprache, schwere Sprache." ("German language, difficult language.") If you are new to German, you may not be familiar with this expression often used by Germans themselves. The language is indeed difficult, but it is not impossible. I am not a native speaker. This book arose from my love of this *schwere Sprache*, frustration at navigating its complexities, and goal of simplifying them for other students by focusing mainly on German nouns. This book takes a nuts-and-bolts approach to the language, emphasizing practical details rather than broad concepts. That makes *Noun Hear This!* a companion handbook to learning German.

## ATTRIBUTES OF GERMAN

German is simpler than other languages in some ways. Unlike languages such as Japanese, which has three different alphabets, German uses the same alphabet as English, plus a few extras (an umlaut on *ä*, *ö*, and *ü*, as well as the double-*s* character *ß*). It is a phonetic language. Unlike many English and French words, German words have spelling and pronunciation that predictably match. There are no spelling bees in Germany! German speakers don't have issues like my French-speaking friend who once asked me what "record" meant. The sentence that troubled him recommended moving a data record ("rec-erd"), but he only knew the word record ("ree-cord") as a verb and was understandably confused about how one moves a "ree-cord." Thankfully, that type of confusion does not happen with German.

Nonetheless, German nouns are complicated compared to English. German adds an element of grammatical gender (masculine, feminine, or neuter) to nouns, while English does not. English has one definite article (*the*); German has six (*der, die, das, den, dem,* and *des*). To choose the correct article for a noun, you must know the noun's gender and its case, which is its function in the sentence. Together, a noun's gender and case can also affect its pronouns and the endings for its adjectives as well as for the noun itself sometimes.

In English, we need to remember only one version of *the table*, for instance. We're lucky that way. We'll go into details later, but for now just watch what happens to the definite article in German here: *The table falls* is *der Tisch fällt.* If you go *behind the table*, you go *hinter den Tisch*, and going *towards the table* is *zu dem Tisch*. If you talk about the *legs of the table*, they are *Beine des Tisches.*

With German, remembering the gender of each noun, considering its function in the sentence, and choosing the correct ending for each adjective is daunting. As a student, I was in a hurry to learn the meanings of words and paid little attention to the nouns' gender. Shame on me, as it kept my language skills weak. If a German noun is masculine, like *Tisch*, but students guess its gender and use the rules for feminine nouns instead, everyone notices the error. It's as obvious as someone saying in English, *I am walked to the car* instead of *I have walked to the car*. People catch the drift, but they may struggle to understand.

## ATTRIBUTES OF THIS BOOK

That is where this book comes in! It aims to make learning less *schwer* by grouping over 2,000 German nouns by gender and color-coding them to support visual learning. It also provides the nouns' English translations and explains their associated grammar. The primary focus is the gender of nouns, followed by their grammar and then their meanings, in that order.

Previously, most dictionaries have focused simply on defining words and have listed them alphabetically without regard for gender. While these materials did not ignore gender, they did not emphasize it, and students had to figure out for themselves how to recall gender details. Even in today's popular language-learning app Duolingo (shown at right), when students are asked for the meaning of words, the app does not display the articles along with the nouns.

Because visual cues help many learners, the dictionary part of this book arranges German nouns by gender and color-codes them accordingly. Think of sports teams wearing jerseys of different colors. It's easy to see which player represents which team. Likewise, you may remember a certain noun's masculine gender more easily by recalling that it was colored red in the *Der* section, which can make speaking and writing German less daunting.

The dictionary in this book focuses on the nouns' definite articles and makes only a minimal attempt to clarify the more obvious distinctions of meaning. It is not intended to provide nuanced definitions. Detecting nuance in language takes time, exposure, and experience. There are many dictionaries online and in print, as well as discussion boards on distinctions of meaning, which provide the depth that *Noun Hear This!* does not. In some cases, words have multiple meanings that are quite distinct. In English, for example, *volume* can indicate space in a container or an attribute of sound. When multiple meanings in German are most distinct, I have attempted to distinguish them. See the "Introduction to the Dictionary" chapter for more details.

The definitions here were produced and checked—translated primarily from English to German and then checked again from German to English—using several sources, including Google and Bing translations, Dict.cc, Leo.org, and others. In search engines, the expression "What is the difference between Word_X and Word_Y in German?" yielded fruitful results. For example, the word for *guilt*, *die Schuld*, is also the word for *debt*, *die Schuld*. *Schuld* can also be used to mean *your fault*, as in *deine Schuld* or *Du hast Schuld*. With some words, I have received different translations from different dictionaries. The dictionary in this book is not meant to be complete but is, as we say in America, "in the ballpark." Where it provides only one translation of a word, this does not mean that no other translations exist.

Like the dictionary, the grammar discussion is intended for the convenience of students who already have some understanding of German. It is written in a narrative style, as if a teacher were talking with a student, meant more as a companion to prior learning than as a starting point for beginners (unless their instructors deem otherwise). The book also contains a glossary and other quick references in the Appendix. This book was developed without the use of AI.

# 2

# REVIEW

## BASIC PARTS OF SPEECH

For simple definitions of grammatical terms and abbreviations, see the "Glossary" section in the Appendix.

### *NOUNS: SUBJECTS AND OBJECTS*

A noun (a *Substantiv* in German) is a person, place, or thing. In German, unlike English, all nouns are assigned a grammatical gender and have their first letter capitalized. Not all nouns are equal, though. **Nouns that are not the subject of a sentence are objects; objects can be either direct or indirect.**

Subjects are nouns that perform actions, such as *bird* in *The bird flies*, *tree* in *the tree falls*, or *he* in *He throws the ball*. Objects are the nouns that are not used as subjects in the sentence, such as *ball* in the last example.

The object being acted upon by the subject is the direct object (DO). In *He throws the ball*, the word *ball* is the DO. In *He eats the cake and will drink the coffee*, the words *cake* and *coffee* are the DOs. You can identify the DOs by asking "What?" What is being consumed? The cake and coffee.

The object that receives the DO, or the object to whom or for whom the subject's action is done, is the indirect object (IO). In *He gives the boy the cake*, the word *boy* is the IO. You can identify the IO by asking "To (or for) whom?" To whom is the cake given? The boy.

### PRONOUNS

A pronoun is a word that is used to replace a noun and avoid repetition. The word to which the pronoun refers is called its antecedent, which must be identified clearly in any language. We cannot use a pronoun without first using a proper or common noun. If I walk into your office and simply announce, "It is brown," you will have no idea what I mean. However, if I say, "I baked a cake last night. It is brown," you will know exactly what *it* is and what item is brown. *Cake* is the antecedent.

### CASES

It is common to state that a noun functions as (or serves as or is termed as) a role—the role of subject, direct object, indirect object, or owner of another noun. **A noun's function in the sentence determines its case.** Recognizing the case is half of the requirement for using nouns successfully. The other half is knowing their gender, and thankfully a noun's gender does not change.

### ARTICLES: DEFINITE AND INDEFINITE

There are two kinds of articles, definite and indefinite (*bestimmter* and *unbestimmter* in German).

In English, the definite article is *the*. When I ask you to hand me *the bottle*, I am being definite, and you know which bottle I mean, especially if I am pointing at it. The indefinite articles are *a* and *an*. When I ask you to hand me *a bottle* or *an egg*, it is understood as any bottle or egg—perhaps a beer bottle, wine bottle, brown egg, green egg, etc.

In English, the same articles are used whether they precede a subject, direct object, or indirect object—in other words, regardless of the noun's function. In German, though, the noun's gender and case affect its articles.

## BASIC WORD ORDER

Before we dig into nouns and their genders, let's review basic German sentence structure. We'll look more closely at word order in our study of the dative case, but **generally, word order is Subject + Verb + More Nouns + More Verbs.**

**The king of all rules is this: The verb always comes in the second place.** When general rules bump into this rule, the king wins! For example, *to thank* is *danken. The man thanks the professor* is *Der Mann dankt dem Professor*, where the subject is *der Mann* and the verb *dankt* is in second place (not the second word). With an adverb at the beginning, *Now the man thanks the professor* is *Nun dankt der Mann dem Professor*. The verb *dankt* maintains second place and *der Mann* moves in accommodation.

# 3

# GENDER

Unlike in English, gender matters greatly in German, and the importance of getting it precisely right cannot be overstated.

Centuries ago, Germans assigned a grammatical gender to each noun and then decided that different genders deserved different definite and indefinite articles. (Of course languages evolve over time and adapt to common usage.) The genders are masculine (M), feminine (F), neuter (N), and plural (P), sometimes abbreviated as MFNP. In German, they are called *männlich*, *weiblich*, *sächlich*, and *plural*. Although plural is not exactly a gender, but is more accurately called a number, we will treat it like a gender here to simplify the logic and minimize terms. When a singular noun becomes plural, its plural status trumps its original gender.

How do you know whether a noun is M, F, or N? Dictionaries provide the gender and then you memorize the association! That's where this book helps. Memorizing and recalling the gender of each noun is a CRITICAL task, one that prevents guessing about which articles to use, among other things.

## DECLENSION

However, knowing a noun's gender is not the ONLY task. A noun's case can also affect its articles as well as other parts of speech. To determine which article to use with a noun, you must:

1. Identify the gender of the noun.
2. Identify the noun's function (the case) in the sentence.

Knowing the gender of a noun is just the beginning, the foundation from which adjectives are built. To summarize, let this be called the Golden Rule of Nouns and Adjectives: **A noun's gender and case determine its articles, pronouns, and endings for its adjectives (as well as for the noun itself sometimes).** This process of changing word forms helps indicate the noun's role in the sentence and is known as declension.

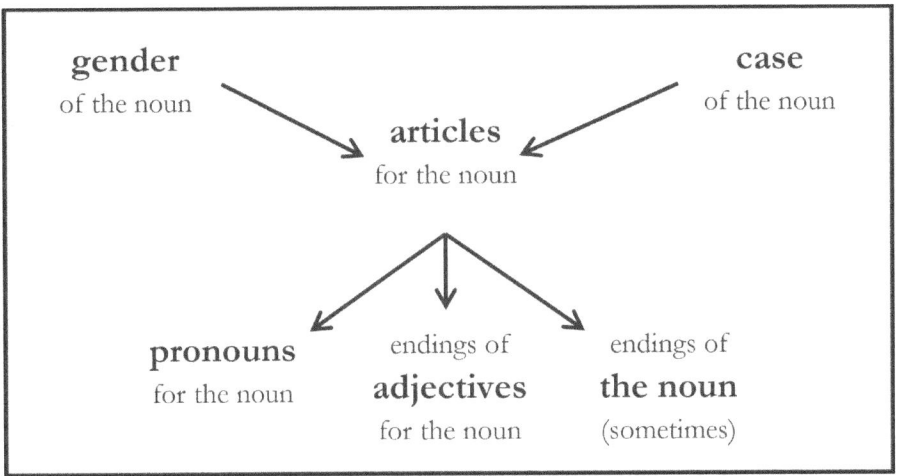

Let the rule above germinate, especially if this is your first introduction to genders and cases. Put the book down, take a break, repeat the rule out loud, and let it settle into your psyche. Then come back and continue.

## EFFECTS ON ARTICLES

This chapter will focus mainly on the definite articles, while later chapters will expand on other topics.

The definite articles (versions of *the*) are *der, die, das, den, dem,* and *des,* which are pronounced dare, dee, doss, dain, dame, and dess. (The International Phonetic Association publishes a method of writing sounds phonetically, but since few understand it, forgive my rebel spellings.) In addition to stating "that word is masculine," it is common to say, "That is a *Der* word" (or *Die* word or *Das* word). The plural is easily recognized, and no guessing is required, because it applies to any quantity of more than one regardless of gender. Happily, there is only MFN singular and not also MFN plural as with Latin!

The base form of the indefinite article is *ein*, which means *a/an/any*. Adding a *k-* in front of it makes *kein* (*no/not any*). Other letters added in front of *ein* indicate possession, such as in *mein*, *dein*, and *sein*. Gender, number (singular or plural), and case determine whether or not an ending is added, and all of the resulting words are referred to as *Ein* words.

Every German noun has one of the following genders and—in the nominative case—the corresponding articles.

|  | Masculine (M) Gender | Feminine (F) Gender | Neuter (N) Gender | Plural (P) |
|---|---|---|---|---|
| **Definite Article** | der | die | das | die |
| **Indefinite Article** | ein | eine | ein | keine |

Now do this: Creating a matrix with five columns and five rows, as shown below, write the three genders and plural across the column headers as M, F, N, and P. Write the four cases (nominative, accusative, dative, and genitive) down the row headers as NOM, ACC, DAT, and GEN. You should have 16 empty boxes for the noun forms, which are combinations of gender and case. Only one of the six definite articles fits into each box; only one version of *the* is correct. In the next chapter, we'll discover which version goes into each box!

|  | M | F | N | P |
|---|---|---|---|---|
| **NOM** |  |  |  |  |
| **ACC** |  |  |  |  |
| **DAT** |  |  |  |  |
| **GEN** |  |  |  |  |

## RULES ABOUT THE GENDER OF NOUNS

A word's gender is usually not apparent, although there are some exceptions.

- *The man*, who is *der Mann*, is obviously masculine, just as *the woman*, who is *die Frau*, is feminine.
- Regarding professions, words that end with *-er* are also masculine. For example, *der Lehrer* means *the male teacher*, and *die Lehrerin* means *the female teacher*. English does not make this distinction; we just call all male and female teachers *teacher*.

## CLUES THAT POINT TO MASCULINE GENDER

There are other clues to the gender of nouns in German. Please note that I used the word "clues," because not all of them are "rules."

- Generally, most nouns that end with *-er* are masculine.
- Generally, so are most nouns that end with *-ismus*, *-el*, or *-ich*, such as *Buddhismus (Buddhism)*, *Löffel (spoon)*, and *Teppich (carpet)*.
- Because *Tag* is a *Der* word, all the days of the week (*Montag, Dienstag*, etc., including *Mittwoch*) are *Der* words. Dates, days, months, and seasons are *Der* words.
- So are locations and directions on a map. *Norden (north)*, *Süden (south)*, *Osten (east)*, and *Westen (west)* are masculine.
- The brand of car you drive is also masculine, as in (accusative singular) *Fahren Sie lieber einen Ford oder einen Benz?*
- Although it is NOT a rule, many one-syllable nouns are *Der* words. It's true for *der Krieg*, *der Ball*, and *der Zug* but not *die Uhr*, *das Land*, or *das Kind*.

### N-DECLENSION

You will soon recognize that German has more guidelines for masculine nouns in the accusative, dative, and genitive cases than in the nominative case. One guideline is called the N-Declension (*N-Deklination* in German). We might as well introduce it now. It says that *-n* or *-en* gets added to the end of the noun when the noun:

- Is masculine and singular
- Is in the accusative, dative, or genitive case
- Is a person or animal
- Has a plural form that ends in *-n* or *-en*

There are exceptions, of course. Some words that meet all conditions above will not follow the N-Declension (and I don't know why), and some words that are not people or animals do follow it, such as *dem Herzen*. We'll look at examples of N-Declension by case later, but be aware of this rule as you read about the cases. For now, just remember that some masculine nouns will have an *-n* or *-en* added at the end.

## CLUES THAT POINT TO FEMININE GENDER

There are more *Die* words in German than any other type, followed by *Der* words. Here are some clues to help identify *Die* words.

- For a change, there is a rule, not just a guideline: Nouns that end with *-eit*, namely *-keit* and *-heit*, are always feminine. Hooray for a rule! This is how some adjectives and adverbs can become nouns. *Langsam* (*slow*) becomes *Langsamkeit* (*slowness*). Most famously, *gesund* (*healthy*) becomes the post-sneeze response of *Gesundheit* (*Health*)! *Die Langsamkeit, die Gesundheit*.
- It is rare, but some words that end with *-e* can attach *-it* at the end. You probably think they fit this *-eit* rule, but you would be wrong. Not to worry; this situation is rare!
- Most nouns that end with *-ung* are feminine, such as *die Meinung* (*the meaning* or *the opinion*). There are many of them, because this is the primary way of making a verb into a noun. *Erwarten* (*to expect*) becomes *die Erwartung* (*the expectation*). *Meinen* (*to mean*) can be used as *Er meint das* (*He means that*) and also *Das ist seine Meinung* (*That is his opinion*).

- Many nouns end with *-schaft* or *-tät*, such as *die Mannschaft* and *die Qualität*. They are feminine.
- Additional nouns with *-ei* endings, such as *Metzgerei* and *Bäckerei*, take the feminine article. So do those ending with *-ik*, *-enz*, *-anz*, or *-ion*, such as *die Politik, die Frequenz, die Distanz,* and *die Religion.*

Some will point out that nouns ending with *-e* are often feminine, but the pattern is much too loose and inconsistent for me to recommend it as a guideline (as with *der Ahne, der Kaffee, der Kollege,* and *das Ende*). It's true that many more nouns ending with *-e* are *Die* words than *Der* or *Das* words. Many masculine nouns do end with *-e*, though, such as *der Löwe, der Junge, der Glaube, der Affe,* and *der Name*. They fall into the category of "weak nouns" (meaning they need help at the end) and will require an *-n* or *-en* suffix in the accusative, dative, and genitive cases and plural forms, as in *Ich habe den Löwen gesehen.* These masculine "weak nouns" are part of the previously mentioned N-Declension. You can read more about them elsewhere. Remember, many words that end in *-e* are feminine, but certainly not all, so be cautious!

## CLUES THAT POINT TO NEUTER GENDER

Moving into the world of neuter nouns, identified by *Das*, we find more rules and guidelines.

- First, a rule: Words that end with *-chen* or *-lein* are diminutive versions of the original noun, the equivalent of the English *-ette* or *-ling. Der Baum (the tree)* becomes *das Bäumchen (the sapling;* note the addition of the umlaut on the first vowel) when you add the *-chen* suffix, and the word becomes neuter. *Die Frau* becomes *das Fräulein (the young woman)*. In speaking, it is not uncommon for Germans to prefer the *-lein* version of making things smaller, and the *-chen* version is often used more in writing. I've not surveyed this preference and have no documentation, but it is my experience. *Häuslein* and *Häuschen (small house)* are both acceptable, as are *Schätzlein* and *Schätzchen (sweetheart or darling)*. In dialects, you'll often hear the *-lein* spoken merely as *-le*, such as *Häusle* and *Schätzle*. Try interchanging *-chen* and *-lein* with your German friends; they'll let you know what is usual for everyday use. However, *pas auf* (*pay attention*)! There are regular German nouns that end with *-chen* that are not diminutive! *Der Kuchen* (*the cake*) is one. *Das Küchlein* describes a small cake. Perhaps you noticed that the first vowel in *Kuchen* does not have an umlaut as required for diminution, like with *Mädchen*. That absence of the umlaut is a clue to stick with the assigned gender and not change it to *das*. The *-chen* is also pronounced differently.

- The nouns for all languages are *Das* words.
- Most nouns that begin with *Ge-* or end with *-um*, *-ium*, or *-ment* are *Das* words.

It would be simpler if foreign words adopted into German (a practice I dislike) assumed the neuter assignment, but they do not. We say *der Computer*, *der Laptop* (but it is acceptable to say *das Laptop*; I have no explanation), and *die Playstation* or *die PS3*, but we also say *das Baby*.

## GUIDELINES FOR PLURALS

Germans decided centuries ago that all plural nouns would adopt *die* as their article in the nominative and accusative cases. All plurals occupying the dative case in a sentence require *den*, and the genitive case requires *der*. The nouns themselves can also change when used in the plural form. When?

- Generally, most masculine nouns add an *-e*. *Der Bleistift* singular becomes *die Bleistifte*. But this is not a rule, just a guideline.
- Nouns that add an *-e* to become plural and have *a*, *o*, or *u* vowels require an umlaut over the first vowel, such as *Knöpfe* (*buttons*) and *Würste* (*sausages*).
- Nouns that end with *-e*, whether M, F, or N, often add an *-n* to the end. *Die Frau* becomes *die Frauen*, for example.
- Generally, most feminine nouns add an *-n* or *-en*.
- Neuter nouns often add an *-er*. *Das Kind* becomes *die Kinder*. *Das Ei* becomes *die Eier*. Words that already end with *-chen*, *-el*, *-en*, or *-er* do not add an ending or an umlaut. *Das Brötchen* becomes *die Brötchen*;

*der Löffel, die Löffel; das Erdbeben, die Erdbeben; der Messer, die Messer;* but *der Auster* becomes *die Austern*, so *pas auf (pay attention)*!

- Nouns that end with any vowel except *-e* usually add an *-s* to become plural (but not *Frau*). *Das Baby, die Babys; die Disco, die Discos;* etc.
- Plurals of abbreviations also add an *-s*.
- So do foreign-adopted words such as *DVDs* and *Sofas*.

## MASTERING GENDER

Most of the clues related to gender are general guidelines, not rules. The only way to be certain is to memorize the gender of words or use them so frequently they become part of your vocabulary. Using words is recommended; *Übung macht den Meister!* Or, as we say, *practice makes perfect.* "Use a word three times, and it's yours!"

Progressing in your knowledge of German will reinforce how essential it is to know the gender of nouns. You may ask, as with the chicken-and-egg question, "Which comes first (and determines the other)—the gender or the definite article?" Maybe both, in a way. In the nominative case, *Der* words are masculine; M words require *der*. *Die* words are feminine; F words require *die*. *Das* words are neuter; N words require *das*. These definite articles, by way of designating gender, also set the rules for the indefinite articles.

# 4

## COMPOUND NOUNS

German can be described as a modular language, more so than English. For example, *potato salad* is two words in English but only one, *Kartoffelsalat*, in German. Think of train boxcars in a German railyard where the boxcars are nouns, and you can connect them to form a new compound noun. For example, German combines three words—*Panzer* (*armor*), *Kampf* (*struggle*), and *Wagen* (*vehicle*)—to come up with their word *Panzerkampfwagen*, which in English we call a *tank*. The original three German nouns are all masculine *Der* words, so, predictably, *der Panzerkampfwagen* is too.

What happens when words of different genders are joined together? There is a rule. *Ja, Ordnung muss sein!* Whichever word is the caboose decides the gender of the new word. In English, we have *housekey*, and its article does not change. In German, *das Haus* is combined with *der Schlüssel* to become *der Hausschlüssel*. Let's look at another example. *Die Last* means *the load* or *the burden*. *Die Kraft* means *power*. *Der Wagen* existed before automobiles and was commonly used to describe a carriage, cart, or, not surprisingly, a wagon. (*Wagen* is also used to describe the Big Dipper, *Der große Wagen*, by the way.) Today, *Wagen* is widely used to mean *vehicle* or *car*. *Die Last, die Kraft, der Wagen*. Join those boxcars, and the rule specifies that the article of the last word wins, so we arrive at *der Lastkraftwagen*, literally *loadpowervehicle* in English, or what we know as a *truck* in the US or a *lorry* in the UK.

Using this modular boxcar capability, all kinds of words can be combined to produce new words, which explains why German has some very long words.

Two words, *der Fuß* (*the foot*) and *der Ball* (*the ball*) combine to form *Fußball* (*football*, which in the US we call *soccer*). With *Fußball*, all kinds of words can be constructed, such as *das Fußballtor* (*soccer goal*, where *das Tor* means *the gate*), *das Fußballtornetz* (*soccer net*), *der Fußballschuh* (*soccer shoe*), *der Fußballplatz* (*soccer pitch* or *soccer place*), *der Fußballverein* (*soccer club*), *der Fußballtrainer* (*male soccer coach*), *die Fußballtrainerin* (*female soccer coach*), and more.

# 5

## CASES

German has cases (*Fälle*), four of them (*vier deutsche Fälle*). In comparison, English has only two cases, the nominative and the objective, and few native speakers are aware of them. What is a case? Think of it as a category related to a noun's or pronoun's role in the sentence. The German cases are:

- Nominative (*Nominativ*)—the subject of a sentence
- Accusative (*Akkusativ*)—the direct object (DO) within a sentence
- Dative (*Dativ*)—the indirect object (IO) within a sentence
- Genitive (*Genitive*)—the owner of a noun

A noun's singular gender category does not change. However, the role a noun or pronoun performs in a sentence affects its case and can, therefore, change its articles, among other parts of speech. German has rules about how these forms change through the cases, which are called declension. We're going to look at these rules next. In the 16-box matrix you drew earlier, think of starting at the top with the nominative case and then descending through the cases, observing how the articles change. That is a declension.

If you have studied other languages with cases, you are ahead of the game, and if you've studied Latin, you will be pleased to know that German has two fewer cases than Latin! Also, be aware that Latin texts often list the cases as the sequence NOM, GEN, ACC, DAT. If you go online, watch videos, or look at other texts, be mindful because different instructors use a different declension order than this text. I've even seen videos online rearranging the gender order as MNF. *Pas auf!* Here our order is MFNP for gender and NOM, ACC, DAT, GEN for the cases.

It's important to remember that **direct objects are in the accusative case, and indirect objects are in the dative case.** A helpful way to remember this is to imagine the alphabet written horizontally. If you put your index finger on D (for direct), put your pinky finger on I (for indirect), and then slide your hand left across the alphabet, your finger that was on D will reach A (for accusative) before the other finger does, meaning that direct objects are associated with the accusative case. Direct objects are accusative (DOA). Now onward to declining articles and adjectives through all the cases!

## NOMINATIVE CASE

For our first example, let's look at the sentence *The man gives* (gifts). (In English, we *give* gifts; in German, they *schenken* gifts. In fact, something that has been *"schenked"* is a *Geschenk*, something gifted. Be careful with *gift*, though, as *das Gift* in German means *the poison*. The man could also *give* an object that is not a gift, as in giving the salt and pepper at a meal. Germans do not "gift" the salt and pepper at dinner; these items are given.) In English, *the man* who gives is the sentence's subject. In German, subjects require the nominative case. As you know, the nominative versions of *the* are *der* for masculine, *die* for feminine, *das* for neuter, and *die* for plural. *Der Mann, die Frau, das Kind, die Männer, die Frauen, die Kinder* (or *ein Mann, eine Frau, ein Kind* for indefinite articles). Our first example is the nominative; *The man gives* (a gift) or *The man gifts* is *Der Mann schenkt.* That's pretty simple and self-explanatory, is it not?

|       | M   | F   | N   | P   |
| ----- | --- | --- | --- | --- |
| **NOM** | der | die | das | die |
| **ACC** |     |     |     |     |
| **DAT** |     |     |     |     |
| **GEN** |     |     |     |     |

## ACCUSATIVE CASE

Our second sentence, which takes us to the accusative case, is *The man gifts the cake*. The man remains the subject, but this time he's gifting something—the cake—directly, so the cake is the direct object (DO). (There are more tests to determine whether a noun functions as a DO, and because the distinction becomes more apparent when discussed with dative prepositions, we will save that for later.) In German, the DO is in the accusative case. You can remember that direct objects are accusative by remembering the abbreviation DOA (Direct Objects are Accusative). Luckily, only masculine nouns change their article in the accusative. *Der* in the nominative becomes *den* in the accusative. Feminine, neuter, and plural remain unchanged. *Den, die, das, die. Kuchen (cake)* is masculine, so we have *Der Mann schenkt den Kuchen*. If he gifts something feminine, neuter, or plural, he would gift *die, das,* or *die*. Examples are *Der Mann schenkt die Farbe (The man gifts the paint)* and *Der Mann schenkt das Gemälde (The man gifts the painting)*.

|        | **M** | **F** | **N** | **P** |
|--------|-------|-------|-------|-------|
| **NOM** | der   | die   | das   | die   |
| **ACC** | den   | die   | das   | die   |
| **DAT** |       |       |       |       |
| **GEN** |       |       |       |       |

### *N-DECLENSION IN THE ACCUSATIVE*

Here are N-Declension examples in the accusative: *Der Präsident (the president). Für den Präsidenten (for the president). Der Junge (the boy). Ich sehe den Jungen (I see the boy). Der Glaube (the belief). Ohne den Glauben (without the belief). Der Glaube* is an example that is not a person/animal.

### *PREPOSITIONS THAT REQUIRE THE ACCUSATIVE*

There are prepositions that remove the effort in deciding which case rules to follow. These prepositions require (as rules, not guidelines) the accusative case. Anytime a noun is preceded by the following prepositions, the accusative case is required. Repeating these German prepositions quickly out loud creates a rhythm that will be easy to memorize as *durch für gegen ohne um*.

*durch (through), für (for), gegen (against), ohne (without), um (around)*

Some examples of their usage: *Ich spaziere durch den Wald (I walk through the forest). Ich arbeite für den Mann (I work for the man). Ich bin gegen den Krieg (I am against the war). Der Drachen fliegt ohne den Wind (The kite flies without the wind).*

Technically, *bis (until)* is also an accusative preposition, but it is often used without an article or with another preposition. Examples: *bis Morgen (until tomorrow)*; *bis auf (except for)*, as in *bis auf den volle Zug (except for the full train)*; and *bis zu*, where *zu* takes the dative case, as in *bis zum nächsten Mal (until the next time)*.

### VERBS THAT REQUIRE THE ACCUSATIVE

Several verbs always require the accusative. Lists are published elsewhere, but some frequently used verbs of this type are the following.

*backen (bake), bekommen (receive), besuchen (visit), bezahlen (pay), einladen (invite), essen (eat), haben (have), hören (hear), kaufen (buy), lernen (learn), lesen (read), machen (make), mögen (like), öffnen (open), rufen (call), schließen (close), sehen (see), trinken (drink), wählen (choose)*

## DATIVE CASE

When there is a direct object (DO), a sentence might also contain an indirect object (IO). However, an IO can be present without a DO. In *The man gifts the cake to the boy*, the boy is the IO (the one to or for whom something is done), automatically placing him in the dative case.

When a noun serves as the IO in the dative case, the versions of *the* (whether M, F, N, or P) change. *Der* in the nominative becomes *dem* in the dative. *Die* becomes *der*. *Das* becomes *dem*. Plural *die* becomes *den*.

In our example of the man gifting the cake to the boy, *Junge* is considered a "weak masculine" noun, a masculine noun that ends with *-e*, so it too changes. It gains the suffix *-n* (perhaps strengthening the noun), becoming *dem Jungen* in the dative. *Der Mann schenkt dem Jungen den Kuchen.*

There's more! In the dative plural, nouns must also have the *-n* suffix. Nothing more gets added if there is already an *-n* at the end of the word.

In dative, *die Frauen* becomes *den Frauen* and *die Männer* becomes *den Männern*. *Das Kind* becomes *den Kindern* in dative plural.

|  | **M** | **F** | **N** | **P** |
|---|---|---|---|---|
| **NOM** | der | die | das | die |
| **ACC** | den | die | das | die |
| **DAT** | dem | der | dem | den (noun +*n*) |
| **GEN** |  |  |  |  |

### N-DECLENSION IN THE DATIVE

In addition to the -*n* ending in the dative plural, the N-Declension rule also applies. Examples are *der Franzoser* (*the Frenchman*) and *mit dem Franzosen* (*with the Frenchman*). *Der Wille* (*the will*, as in commitment) becomes *dem Willen* in dative. The -*n* gets added to these singular masculine nouns.

### IMPLIED PREPOSITIONS

Dative implies the presence of *zu* (*to*) or *mit* (*with*), and those prepositions are not necessarily required. An example—*DEM DEUTSCHEN VOLKE* (*TO THE GERMAN PEOPLE*)—is displayed in Berlin on the portico of the building for the German parliament, *Der Bundestag*, as shown here.

(In *Bundestag*, *Bundes* means *federal*. Although *Tag* means *day*, it also meant *diet*, referring not to nutritional consumption but to days of work or a designated voting assembly. Somehow it mingled with the Latin *dies* for *days*, and the etymology declares that is how it became to be called a *Tag*. Perhaps you have heard of the Diet of Augsburg or the Diet of Worms from the Middle Ages, before Bismarck unified Germany into a country in 1871. Did you notice the -*E* added to *VOLK* in the inscription? German grammar once required adding an -*e* to nouns in the dative case, a practice that has since stopped. That's why the inscription is not *DEM DEUTSCHEN VOLK*.)

## PREPOSITIONS THAT REQUIRE THE DATIVE

As with the accusative case, prepositions make it simpler to identify the dative case. The following prepositions are some of those that require the dative case.

*aus (out of, from), außer (besides, except), bei (next to, by, with), mit (with), nach (towards, after, according to), seit (since), von (from, of, by), zu (to)*

In the sentence *Ich gehe mit dem Kind nach der Schweiz* (*I go with the child to Switzerland*), *mit* and *nach* both dictate that *das Kind* and *die Schweiz* require the dative articles and become *dem Kind* and *der Schweiz*.

### VERBS THAT REQUIRE THE DATIVE

Additionally, it will help you in your practice to know verbs that require the dative case. The following verbs are some examples.

*antworten (answer), danken (thank), dienen (serve), folgen (follow), gefallen (please), gehören (belong to), glauben (believe), helfen (help), zustimmen (agree to)*

Some examples of their usage: *Er hilft dem Hund. Sie antwortet der Frau. Das Auto gehört dem Mädchen* (*The car belongs to the girl*). *Die Blumen gefallen den Gegnern* (*The flowers please the opponents*). *Ich stimme dir zu* (*I agree with you*).

## CASES AND WORD ORDER

**Gender does not affect word order, but case does!** Changing the case can also change the meaning of a sentence even when word order stays the same.

Word order in German does not always mirror English. If we only understood *dem*, *der*, or *den* as a solitary *the* without regard to noun function (case) and relied solely on word order, we could incorrectly translate the sentence *Den Kuchen schenkt der Mann dem Jungen* into English as *The cake gifts the man the boy*. In English, with only one *the*, word order is everything, but applying this understanding to German would wreck the translation. We know a cake gifts nothing (calories are not gifts)! In *Der Mann schenkt dem Jungen den Kuchen*, the dative implies the existence of *to* or *with*, as in the Bundestag inscription.

When a noun is in the accusative or dative case, the usual order of the More Nouns section of the sentence is broken down further into Subject (in nominative case) + Verb + More Nouns (in dative and accusative case, with their associated adjectives) + More Verbs. **When the More Nouns section includes both a DO and IO, the order for noun cases becomes Nominative + Dative + Accusative (NDA)**, which you can remember by using the initialism for a non-disclosure agreement as a mnemonic. (There is a variation in this word order when pronouns appear, which we will cover soon.)

Here's what's cool about German or other languages with cases: You can figure out who is doing what to/with whom, without depending on word order, just by knowing which noun is accusative and which is dative! In German, the sentence *Der Mann schenkt dem Jungen den Kuchen* (literally, *The man gifts to the boy the cake* in English) has the same meaning as *Den Kuchen schenkt der Mann dem Jungen* (literally, *The cake gifts the man the boy* in English). The word order in the second example might be silly, but in German, there is no doubt about what role each noun plays! The boy is still the receiver, the "to whom" the cake is given; the man remains the doer, the subject, the *Substantiv*; and the cake remains the DO. The clarifying or triggering prepositions such as *to*, *with*, *for*, and *through* are helpful but not required. (I recommend using them, though.)

Let's try a plural version. *Die Männer schenken den Jungen* (which can also be *den Jungs*) *die Kuchen* is, literally, *The men gift to the boys the cakes* in English. The word order is Subject + Verb + IO + DO with cases in the order of NDA. (Don't be confused because *den* can also be the masculine accusative. The *-en* or *-s* ending signals that *Jungen* or *Jungs* is plural.) With the nominative plural subject *men*, plural verb *gift*, dative plural IO *to the boys*, and accusative plural DO *the cakes*, the case order remains NDA.

**Prepositions clarify case.** Another general rule for word order in German that is worth mentioning is the sequence of time, manner, and place (TMP). *I go to the park on Tuesdays*, when translated to German and then back to English literally, becomes *I go Tuesdays to the park*. In the sentence *Ich gehe mit dem Kind nach der Schweiz* (*I go with the child to Switzerland*), the manner of going is *with the child* and *Switzerland* is a place, so TMP applies and explains why *Ich gehe mit dem Kind nach der Schweiz* instead of *Ich gehe nach der Schweiz mit dem Kind* (*I go to Switzerland with the child*).

You can go a long way in speaking German while knowing only the NDA cases. Before we consider the last case, genitive, let's look at the far more frequent use of pronouns.

# 6

# PRONOUNS BEFORE CONSIDERING GENITIVE CASE

Pronouns (*Personalpronomen* in German) are primarily associated with the nominative, accusative, and dative cases, so we will consider them before digging into the genitive case.

When it comes to pronouns, German maintains its gender designations. Pronouns retain the gender of the nouns they replace, but they also change according to the case (decline in the cases). Correctly choosing the pronoun requires the speaker to know the noun's gender and its role in the sentence!

A big distinction between German and English usage is that English uses *it* for items that are not alive. Not so in German. Instead of being an *it*, the masculine *der Kuchen* becomes a *him*, and the feminine *die Butter* becomes a *her*. *Der Mann schenkt ihn*, referring to the cake, is *The man gives him*. If the man gives the butter instead, *Der Mann schenkt sie*, which means *The man gives her*. It is important to know you cannot simply use *es* (*it*) for all inanimate pronouns.

Pronouns and associated verbs are known as being "in a person." There are three persons—first, second (informal or formal), and third—which can be singular or plural. (When I began to study German, each word for *you* started with a capital letter. Today, only the formal versions of *you* require capitalization as *Sie* or *Ihnen* depending on their case.)

## PRONOUNS IN THE NOMINATIVE CASE

Here is the nominative case, where the noun is a subject performing an action. Note that the second-person formal pronoun begins with a capital letter and takes the verb infinitive. An infinitive is the base form of a verb. In English, it usually includes *to*, such as in *to go*. In German, the infinitive is only one word and it's identified by the *-en* ending, such as in *gehen (to go)*. This verb retains the infinitive form when used with the formal *you* in *Sie gehen (you go)* but has other forms when used with the informal *you* in *du gehst* or other pronouns in *ich gehe (I go)* and *sie geht (she goes)*.

|            | Singular                     | Plural                  |
|------------|------------------------------|-------------------------|
| **1st**    | ich (I)                      | wir (we)                |
| **2nd informal** | du (you)               | ihr (you / y'all)       |
| **2nd formal** | Sie (you)                | Sie (you)               |
| **3rd**    | er, sie, es (he, she, it)    | sie (they)              |

Let's look at the cake that is brown. *Der Kuchen ist braun (The cake is brown)*. To say *it* instead of *the cake* in German, we have already learned to say *Er ist Braun (He is brown)*, because *Kuchen* is masculine. In this example, *er (he)* refers to its antecedent *der Kuchen*. It is incorrect to say, as we would in English, *Es ist braun (It is brown)* when referring to the masculine *der Kuchen*.

The same rule applies to feminine nouns, as in *Die Lampe ist Gelb (The lamp is yellow)*. To substitute *it* for *the lamp* after the first usage, we would say *Sie ist Gelb (She is yellow)*.

For neuter nouns, *es (it)* is accurate. For example, *Das Haus ist klein (The house is small)* becomes *Es ist klein (It is small)*.

See how that works? Some things are *it*; most are *he* or *she*. This distinction changes how an English speaker thinks about pronouns. It's a shift in thinking, but it's not difficult with practice. As we go through this grammar, it reinforces how vital gender is in German!

## PRONOUNS IN THE ACCUSATIVE CASE

Here is the accusative case, where the noun is a DO that receives the verb's action. Note that the second-person formal pronoun begins with a capital letter.

|  | Singular | Plural |
|---|---|---|
| **1st** | mich (me) | uns (us) |
| **2nd informal** | dich (you) | euch (you / y'all) |
| **2nd formal** | Sie (you) | Sie (you) |
| **3rd** | ihn, sie, es (him, her, it) | sie (them) |

Use the verb *verstehen* (*to understand*), and you can piece this together on your own. *Verstehst du mich* (*Do you understand me*)? *Ich verstehe dich* (*I understand you*). *Sie versteht ihn* (*She understands him*). *Er versteht sie* (*He understands her*). *Ich verstehe es* (*I understand it*). *Sie verstehen uns* (*They understand us*). *Ich verstehe euch* (*I understand y'all*).

## PRONOUNS IN THE DATIVE CASE

Here is the dative case, where the noun is an IO to (or for) whom (or which) the verb's action is done. Note that the second-person formal pronoun begins with a capital letter.

|  | Singular | Plural |
|---|---|---|
| **1st** | mir (me) | uns (us) |
| **2nd informal** | dir (you) | euch (you / y'all) |
| **2nd formal** | Ihnen (you) | Ihnen (you) |
| **3rd** | ihm, ihr, ihm (him, her, it) | ihnen (them) |

In the dative, the rule about using *him* and *her* pronouns even for inanimate M or F nouns is the same, but the words for *him* and *her* are different from those in the accusative case, as seen above. The M version of *it* is *ihm* (*him*), the F version of *it* is *ihr* (*her*), and this time the neuter version of *it* also changes to *ihm*. The word for *them* is *ihnen*. *Ihnen* (beginning with a capital letter) is also the formal *you* in the dative. The plural informal *you* remains *euch*. Some examples with singular informal *dir* (*you*) and *mir* (*me*): *Willst du mir etwas schenken* (*Do you want to give me something*)? *Ich schenke dir etwas* (*I give you something*).

## PRONOUNS AND WORD ORDER

Let's look closer at word order when using pronouns. We have already discussed the word order of NDA with noun cases. When using pronouns, the rule is that **the pronoun is placed closer than any nouns to the verb**, regardless of the pronoun's gender, number, or case. The pronoun just has to be closest, not necessarily next to the verb.

*Der Mann schenkt ihm den Kuchen* (*The man gifts him the cake*). In this example, the man gives to a dative pronoun an accusative noun, which aligns with the NdA sequence (with the lowercase *d* indicating a pronoun instead of a noun). However, when *cake* is replaced with the pronoun and the boy returns as a noun, in the sentence *Der Mann schenkt ihn dem Jungen* (*The man gifts it to the boy*), we see how the pronoun stays next to the verb. This time, the man gives an accusative pronoun to a dative noun, and the word order becomes NaD.

When both DO and IO pronouns exist, as in *I gift it to him*, the accusative DO pronoun precedes the dative IO pronoun. The sentence structure changes to **Subject (nominative) + Verb + DO (accusative) + IO (dative), with noun and pronoun cases in the order of Nad.** *Der Mann schenkt ihn ihm* (*The man gave it to him*). However... (Yes, exceptions abound!), if you say, *Now the man gifts it to him*—remembering that the verb ALWAYS comes in the second place and this rule beats all others—the sentence becomes *Nun schenkt der Mann ihn ihm*, with *schenkt* in second place! When this occurs, the DO pronoun, the accusative, stands closest to the subject. *Nun schenkt der Mann ihn dem Jungen* has a case order of Nad.

Prepositions that require the accusative or dative forms for nouns also apply to pronouns. There is another set of prepositions that I call "wishy-washy" (my term, no one else's) because they can be used with either the accusative or dative case. Before we get into the genitive case, let's look at these wishy-washy prepositions.

# 7

# WISHY-WASHY PREPOSITIONS

You have learned prepositions that require the accusative case and ones that require the dative case. There are also wishy-washy prepositions that can function with either of these cases, depending on the verb and the noun. Officially they are called dual case prepositions (*Wechselpräpositionen* in German), but my description is more fun. Don't worry; the usage is not difficult to understand, and it will be even easier if you can memorize these nine prepositions:

> *an (at, to, on;* vertical)*, auf (on, upon, onto), hinter (behind), in (in, into), neben (beside), über (above, over, about), unter (below, under, among), vor (ago, in front of, before), zwischen (between)*

The noun or pronoun you use with these prepositions is going to be either accusative or dative. You need a way of deciphering which declension to use. How to do it? **When there is motion toward an object (i.e., going from one space to another), that noun will be the DO, in the accusative case; otherwise, it will be dative.** That rule determines which case to use with any of the wishy-washy prepositions.

An example is *Sie geht in das Haus* (*She goes in the house*). Compare that to *Sie wohnt in dem Haus* (*She lives in the house*). The difficulty might be deciding what is considered motion. Philosophically, living is constant motion, but someone is not "living" an object to or towards anything. When there is a direction towards an object, then the object is accusative. When *Er erinnert sich an dich* (*He remembers you*), you are the direct object of the memory and thus accusative. Other verbs like *lesen* (*to read*) and *kennen* (*to know*) imply the accusative also. When *Ich gehe hinter das Stadion* (*I walk behind the stadium*), *Stadion* is neuter, so its accusative article *das* is used. *Denken + an, sich freuen + auf* or *über*, and *warten + auf* all require accusative. Examples: *Ich denke an dich. Ich freue mich auf das Geschenk. Ich warte immer auf euch.*

An example of a dative noun with a wishy-washy preposition is *Sie sitzt in dem Auto* (*She is sitting in the car*). There is no motion, right? She's only sitting, so the dative is required.

Memorize those prepositions and practice discovering whether a noun will be accusative or dative. *Die Stadt* (*the city*) is a helpful example. In *Ich gehe in die Stadt* (*I am going into the city*), *die Stadt* is accusative. In *Ich bin in der Stadt* (*I am in the city*), *der Stadt* is dative. (Sometimes I am glad English is my native language!)

Now that we have a solid understanding of pronouns, prepositions, and three cases, let's return to the man giving the boy a cake and continue with adding a noun in the final case, genitive.

# 8

# GENITIVE CASE, ONWARD!

The genitive case is pretty straightforward. It indicates possession or ownership and can generally be associated with the preposition *of*.

The MFNP definite articles for the genitive are *des*, *der*, *des*, *der*. A special thing to remember about the genitive is that masculine and neuter nouns have an *-s* (if the noun ends with a vowel, including *y*) or an *-es* (if the noun ends with a consonant) added to the end. *Der Mann* becomes *des Mannes* (*of the man*), and *das Baby* becomes *des Babys*.

Genitives are often used in writing. You'll see them in the newspaper, magazines, books, etc., and less often in speech. Typically, people say, *Das auto gehört dem Mann* (*The car belongs to the man*). Notice *gehören* (*to belong to*) requires the dative case. In genitive, we would say *das Auto des Mannes* (*the car of the man*). The genitive article indicates *of the*. Other examples include *das Auto der Männer* (*the car of the men*), *das Auto der Frau* (*the car of the woman*), *das Auto der Frauen* (*the car of the women*), *das Auto des Babys*, and *das Auto der Babys*, as well as *Das Dach des Hauses* (*the roof of the house*) and *Das Dach der Häuser* (*the roof of the houses*).

In our example about the cake, let's add a genitive noun. *Der Mann schenkt dem Jungen den Kuchen des Bäckers* (*The man gifts the boy the cake of the baker*, literally). Notice the word order. The item the baker owns, the cake, precedes *des Bäckers*. Shuffled around, the phrase *der Junge des Bäckers* means *the boy of the baker* or *the baker's boy*.

| | M | F | N | P |
|---|---|---|---|---|
| **NOM** | der | die | das | die |
| **ACC** | den | die | das | die |
| **DAT** | dem | der | dem | den (noun +n) |
| **GEN** | des (noun +s/es) | der | des (noun +s/es) | der |

To help remember the articles, say them in four groups of four like this:

- NOM: "der, die, das, die"
- ACC: "den, die, das, die"
- DAT: "dem, der, dem, den"
- GEN: "des, der, des, der"

## N-DECLENSION IN THE GENITIVE

The N-Declension applies also in the genitive case. When *der Franzoser* (*the Frenchman*) becomes *des Franzosens* (*of the Frenchmen*), for example, an *-s* gets added after the additional *-n*.

## PREPOSITIONS THAT REQUIRE THE GENITIVE

Luckily, there are some rules about prepositions that require the genitive case. Some, but not all, of these prepositions are listed here:

*(an)statt (instead of), außerhalb (outside of), beiderseits (mutually, both sides of), diesseits (this side of), infolge (as a result of), innerhalb (within), mithilfe (with the help of), trotz (in spite of), um...willen (for the sake of), während (while, during), wegen (because of)*

Here are examples of genitive prepositions in use: *Anstatt des Autos kaufte er ein Fahrrad (Instead of the car, he bought a bicycle). Wegen des Wetters bleibe ich zu Hause (Because of the weather, I am staying home). Infolge des Unfalls (as a result of the accident). Sie wohnt außerhalb der Stadt (She lives outside the city). Innerhalb der Woche (within the week).*

# 9

# INDEFINITE ARTICLES

Hooray! We got through the definite articles, prepositions, word order, and some verbs that require certain cases. Now that we have looked at how cases affect the endings of definite articles, a matrix with indefinite articles (versions of *a* and *an*) will suffice without an expanded narrative. Remember that, in the nominative case, the indefinite articles are *ein* and *eine*, while *keine* (*no*, as in *not any*) can be used for singular and plural nouns. These indefinite articles are all built on the word *eins* (*one*), but without -*s*, and are in a category known as *Ein* words.

|  | M | F | N | P |
|------|------------------|------|------------------|------------------|
| NOM | ein | eine | ein | keine |
| ACC | einen | eine | ein | keine |
| DAT | einem | einer | einem | keinen (noun +n) |
| GEN | eines (noun +s/es) | einer | eines (noun +s/es) | keiner |

The endings of the indefinite articles match the declension pattern of the definite articles. Easy, right? Until we add adjectives! I highly encourage you to master the article endings before proceeding to adjectives. There will be a lot to remember. If you don't master a topic before moving on, in a few days it becomes mush, a jumble of endings and rules floating around like mashed potatoes in your memory. In contrast, if you master the material we've covered so far, you'll be proud of your progress and better able to keep building on it.

# 10

# ADJECTIVES

Adjectives modify and describe nouns by size, color, shape, age, quantity, opinion, etc. **When adjectives come after a noun and verb, they are simple.** In *Der Kartoffel ist braun* (*The potato is brown*), no letters are added to the end of *braun*.

**When an adjective precedes a noun, though, the adjective declines with the article.** Both the adjective and the article change form accordingly, and you must change the adjective's ending. The changes are determined by the type of article (definite or indefinite) or by the absence of an article. The ending of the adjective must "agree" with the gender and case of the noun. It is forbidden to use a feminine adjective ending with a masculine noun, or a masculine adjective ending with a plural noun, etc. You cannot mix and match; you can only match! We say "the ending agrees with the gender" and the case when we use the ending in the correct matrix box. Yes, it's matrix time again.

A reminder as we again consider the effects of declension: remember that masculine and neuter nouns have *-s* or *-es* added in the genitive case, and plural nouns have *-n* added in the dative case.

In addition, adjectives have endings that are commonly referred to as "strong" or "weak," and they follow these three rules:

- Adjectives without articles have strong endings (which indicate the noun's gender when there is no article to do so).
- Adjectives with definite articles have weak endings.
- Adjectives with indefinite articles have a mix of strong and weak endings.

## ADJECTIVES WITHOUT ARTICLES (STRONG ENDINGS)

*Fresh coffee* is an example. Without an article, the ending of the adjective usually takes the ending of the definite article. There's an exception for masculine and neuter singular nouns in the genitive case; their adjective endings are *-en* instead of *-es* as one might expect. Remember, for nouns that end in *-e*, we do not add an extra *e*. Here are examples of adjectives with strong endings.

|       | M                  | F              | N                | P                  |
|-------|--------------------|----------------|------------------|--------------------|
| **NOM** | frisch-er Kaffee   | gut-e Milch    | kalt-es Wasser   | frisch-e Kaffees   |
| **ACC** | frisch-en Kaffee   | gut-e Milch    | kalt-es Wasser   | frisch-e Kaffees   |
| **DAT** | frisch-em Kaffee   | gut-er Milch   | kalt-em Wasser   | frisch-en Kaffees  |
| **GEN** | frisch-en Kaffees  | gut-er Milch   | kalt-en Wassers  | frisch-er Kaffees  |

## ADJECTIVES WITH DEFINITE ARTICLES (WEAK ENDINGS)

Adjectives with definite articles have endings of *-e* or *-en*. Here are examples of adjectives with these weak endings.

|       | M                 | F               | N                | P                 |
|-------|-------------------|-----------------|------------------|-------------------|
| **NOM** | der kurz-e Urlaub  | die nett-e Frau  | das blau-e Auto   | die nett-en Eltern |
| **ACC** | den kurz-en Urlaub | die nett-e Frau  | das blau-e Auto   | die nett-en Eltern |
| **DAT** | dem kurz-en Urlaub | der nett-en Frau | dem blau-en Auto  | den nett-en Eltern |
| **GEN** | des kurz-en Urlaubs | der nett-en Frau | des blau-en Autos | der nett-en Eltern |

# ADJECTIVES WITH INDEFINITE ARTICLES

When adjectives are added between an indefinite article and noun, the adjectives have a mix of weak and strong endings. Look at the adjective endings below, and you will see some similarities that make recall less formidable. Of the 16 adjectives, 11 take the ending -en. Two take -e, two take -es, and one takes -er.

|  | M | F | N | P |
|---|---|---|---|---|
| **NOM** | ein kurz-er Urlaub | eine nett-e Frau | ein blau-es Auto | deine nett-en Eltern |
| **ACC** | einen kurz-en Urlaub | eine nett-e Frau | ein blau-es Auto | deine nett-en Eltern |
| **DAT** | einem kurz-en Urlaub | einer nett-en Frau | einem blau-en Auto | deinen nett-en Eltern |
| **GEN** | eines kurz-en Urlaubs | einer nett-en Frau | eines blau-en Autos | deiner nett-en Eltern |

This is a good time to pause and make sure you understand the adjective endings. Take a break. Then come back and check that you've memorized these patterns before continuing!

## POSSESSIVE ADJECTIVES

*Yours*, *Mine*, and *Ours* (the name of an old movie) are examples of possessive pronouns, which can stand alone without nouns. Possessive adjectives, such as *your*, *my*, and *our*, precede and modify nouns. In German, some of them end with -*ein* (*mein*, *dein*, and *sein*) and, like the indefinite articles, are in the category of *Ein* words. Other possessive adjectives (*unser*, *euer*, and *ihr*) are not literally *Ein* words, but their endings follow the rules for *Ein* words anyway.

Like pronouns, possessive adjectives come in three persons—first, second (informal or formal), and third—which can be singular or plural. Possessive adjectives also get declined by all the cases. In this declension, their endings match those of the other *Ein* words, the indefinite articles. Instead of going through all the cases, therefore, we will cover just a few examples here. One reminder: remember that the second-person formal possessive adjective always begins with a capital letter.

In the nominative case, possessive adjectives have the following genderless base forms.

|  | Singular | Plural |
|---|---|---|
| **1st** | mein (my) | unser (our) |
| **2nd informal** | dein (your) | euer (your) |
| **2nd formal** | Ihr (your) | Ihr (your) |
| **3rd** | sein, ihr, sein (his, her, its) | ihr (their) |

The following examples show how *unser* gets declined through the cases when used with MFNP nouns.

|  | **M** | **F** | **N** | **P** |
|---|---|---|---|---|
| **NOM** | unser Vater | unser-e Mutter | unser Auto | unser-e Brillen |
| **ACC** | unser-en Vater | unser-e Mutter | unser Auto | unser-e Brillen |
| **DAT** | unser-em Vater | unser-er Mutter | unser-em Auto | unser-en Brillen |
| **GEN** | unser-es Vaters | unser-er Mutter | unser-es Autos | unser-er Brillen |

All the possessive adjectives get declined with the same endings as above, including *euer*. When it precedes a masculine noun, for example, it has the endings *euer*, *eur-en*, *eur-em*, and *eur-es*.

### POSSESSIVE ADJECTIVES IN THE GENITIVE CASE

When used with nouns in the genitive case, possessive adjectives have the following forms, which all end with *-es*, *-er*, *-es*, *-er*. The singular possessive adjectives are below, and the plural possessive adjectives (such as *unser*) have the same endings.

| | **M** | **F** | **N** | **P** |
|---|---|---|---|---|
| **1st** | mein-es Vaters | mein-er Mutter | mein-es Autos | mein-er Brillen |
| **2nd informal** | dein-es Vaters | dein-er Mutter | dein-es Autos | dein-er Brillen |
| **2nd formal** | Ihr-es Vaters | Ihr-er Mutter | Ihr-es Autos | Ihr-er Brillen |
| **3rd** | sein-es /ihr-es/ sein-es Vaters | sein-er/ ihr-er/sein-er Mutter | sein-es/ ihr-es/sein-es Autos | sein-er/ ihr-er/ sein-er Brillen |

## MOVING ON

We have gone through the genders, cases, pronouns, and adjectives to give you a strong start toward mastering everyday conversation and writing. By now, there should be no further need to emphasize the importance of knowing the gender of any noun you choose.

There's still more to know. There are other pronouns called "demonstrative" (*this*, *such*, *these*, *those*, *that one*, *the same as*, etc.), which require adjective endings but are beyond this text's primary focus on the gender of German nouns. You can quickly find discussions of demonstrative pronouns elsewhere. There are also interrogatives. *Wer* (*who*) gets declined in German, becoming *wen* (*for whom*), *wem* (*to whom* or *with whom*), or *wessen* (*whose*). Reflexive pronouns also change as the functions change, compared to English where a simple *who* suffices for all. As with English, adjectives can also become nouns in German. For instance, *der alte Mann* (*the old man*) can become *der Alte*, and *die alte Frau* (*the old woman*) can become *die Alte*.

This part of the text comes to an end, but I encourage you to practice, practice, practice! Speak German when you can. Now and then, when you say or think something, see if you can translate those thoughts into German, and then check yourself with one of the translation apps. The day is coming when you'll start dreaming in German. When it does, you'll know you've accomplished something and are well on your way to proficiency!

# PART II:

# DICTIONARY

# 11

# INTRODUCTION TO THE DICTIONARY

This dictionary contains a German-to-English chapter followed by an English-to-German chapter. While the latter lists all the English nouns alphabetically, the former divides German nouns into *Der* words, *Die* words, and then *Das* words to match the way German genders are normally presented. The dictionary ends with a chapter of proper and special nouns.

All dictionary chapters list the German nouns in their singular forms, which are followed by plural forms if plurals exist. All German nouns are colored according to gender with masculine in red, feminine in blue, neuter in green, and plural in purple.

When referring to a single person, German identifies that person's gender. For example, there is a word for a male teacher and a word for a female teacher, but never just *a teacher*. When presenting words like *teacher*, this dictionary lists them—under "Masculine *(Der)* Nouns"—with the masculine singular noun first, followed by the masculine plural, a semicolon, the feminine singular, and the feminine plural. The female teacher takes the feminine article, adding *-in* to the base word *Lehrer*, while the feminine plural adds *-innen*. The entry looks like this: *Der Lehrer, Die Lehrer; Die Lehrerin, Die Lehrerinnen.*

This dictionary provides general definitions and does not delve into nuance. Other references can satisfy your search for a more detailed understanding. Some words have multiple meanings and therefore multiple entries. For example, *der Drachen* is German for *the dragon*, but Germans also refer to a kite as *der Drachen*, so the dictionary lists this noun twice, associated with both *dragon* and *kite*. A few of the words that have multiple meanings also have different genders for the different meanings, such as *See* in *Die See ist salzig; der See nicht* (*The sea is salty; the lake is not*), but this situation is quite rare.

# 12

# GERMAN TO ENGLISH

## MASCULINE *(DER)* NOUNS

| German | English |
|---|---|
| Der Aal, Die Aale | Eel |
| Der Abbruch, Die Abbrüche | Cancel (such as at an ATM) |
| Der Abbruch, Die Abbrüche | Demolition |
| Der Abend, Die Abende | Evening |
| Der Abfall, Die Abfälle | Garbage |
| Der Abflug, Die Abflüge | Departure (flight) |
| Der Abpfiff, Die Abpfiffe | Whistle, Final |
| Der Abschied, Die Abschiede | Farewell |
| Der Abschied, Die Abschiede | Parting |
| Der Abstand, Die Abstände | Distance |
| Der Abstinenzler, Die Abstinenzler; Die Abstinenzlerin, Die Abstinenzlerinnen | Teetotaler |
| Der Adel | Nobility |
| Der Adler, Die Adler | Eagle |
| Der Agent, Die Agenten; Die Agentin, Die Agentinnen | Agent |
| Der Ahne, Die Ahnen; Die Ahnin, Die Ahninnen | Ancestor |
| Der Aktienmarkt, Die Aktienmärkte | Stock Market |
| Der Aktivismus | Activism |
| Der Albtraum, Die Albträume | Nightmares |
| Der Algorithmus, Die Algorithmen | Algorithm |
| Der Alltag | Everyday Life |
| Der Altist, Die Altisten; Die Altistin, Die Altistinnen | Alto |
| Der Anarchismus | Anarchy |

| German | English |
|---|---|
| Der Anarchist, Die Anarchisten; Die Anarchistin, Die Anarchistinnen | Anarchist |
| Der Anfange, Die Anfänge | Beginning |
| Der Anfänger, Die Anfänger | Beginner |
| Der Anflug, Die Anflüge | Approach |
| Der Angehörige, Die Angehörigen | Member of a Family |
| Der Angeklagte, Die Angeklagten; Die Angeklagten, Die Angeklagtenin | Accused |
| Der Angestellte, Die Angestellten | Employee, Salaried |
| Der Angestellte, Die Angestellten; Die Angestellte, Die Angestellten | Salaried, White-Collar Employee |
| Der Angriff, Die Angriffe | Assault, Offensive |
| Der Anhänger, Die Anhänger; Die Anhängerin, Die Anhängerinnen | Supporter, Backer |
| Der Anker, Die Anker | Anchor |
| Der Ankläger, Die Ankläge; Die Anklägerin, Die Anklägerin | Prosecutor |
| Der Anruf, Die Anrufe | Call |
| Der Anschlag, Die Anschläge | Attack |
| Der Anstieg, Die Anstiege (from *anstiegen*) | Rise |
| Der Anteil, Die Anteile | Portion, Share (of something) |
| Der Anteilseigner, Die Anteilseigner; Die Anteilseignerin, Die Anteilseignerinnen | Shareholder |
| Der Antrag, Die Anträge | Application, Proposal, a Motion |
| Der Anwalt, Die Anwälte; Die Anwältin, Die Anwältinnen | Lawyer |
| Der Anzug, Die Anzüge | Suit |
| Der Apfel, Die Äpfel | Apple |
| Der Apfelsaft, Die Apfelsäfte | Apple Juice |
| Der Apotheker, Die Apotheker; Die Apothekerin, Die Apothekerininnen | Pharmacist |
| Der April | April |
| Der Arbeiter, Die Arbeiter; Die Arbeiterin, Die Arbeiterinnen | Worker, Laborer, Blue-Collar Employee |
| Der Arbeitgeber, Die Arbeitgeber; Die Arbeitgeberin, Die Arbeitgeberinnen | Employer |
| Der Arbeitnehmer, Die Arbeitnehmer; Die Arbeitnehmerin, Die Arbeitnehmerinnen | Employee, Wage Earner |
| Der Arbeitslose, Die Arbeitslosen | Unemployed |
| Der Arbeitsunfall, Die Arbeitsunfälle | Work Accident |
| Der Arbeitsvertrag, Die Arbeitsverträge | Employment Contract |
| Der Arm, Die Arme | Arm |

| German | English |
|---|---|
| Der Ast, Die Äste | Branch, tree |
| Der Atem, Die Atem | Breath |
| Der Atheismus | Atheism |
| Der Atheist, Die Atheisten; Die Atheistin, Die Atheistinnen | Atheist |
| Der Atlantik | Atlantic |
| Der Aufsatz, Die Aufsätze | Essay |
| Der Aufschlag, Die Aufschläge | Markup, Price Increase |
| Der Auftrag, Die Aufträge | Task |
| Der Aufwand, Die Aufwände | Effort |
| Der Aufzug, Die Aufzüge | Elevator |
| Der August | August |
| Der Ausbruch, Die Ausbrüche | Outbreak |
| Der Ausdruck, Die Ausdrücke | Expression |
| Der Ausschuss, Die Ausschüsse | Committee |
| Der Austausch, Die Austausche | Exchange (as in exchange student) |
| Der Ausweis, Die Ausweise | ID Card |
| Der Automat, Die Automaten | Vending Machine |
| Der Autor, Die Autoren; Die Autorin, Die Autorinnen | Author |
| Der Autoreifen, Die Autoreifen | Tire, Car |
| Der Backofen, Die Backöfen | Oven |
| Der Bahnhof, Die Bahnhöfe | Train Station |
| Der Bahnsteig, Die Bahnsteige | Platform (train) |
| Der Bakkalaureus, Die Bakkalaurei | Bachelor's Degree |
| Der Balkon, Die Balkone | Balcony |
| Der Ball, Die Bälle | Ball |
| Der Barsch, Die Barsche | Bass (fish) |
| Der Baseball, Die Baseballs | Baseball |
| Der Basketball, Die Basketbälle | Basketball |
| Der Bass, Die Bässe | Bass (instrument) |
| Der Bassist, Die Bassisten; Die Bassistin, Die Bassistinnen | Bass (person) |
| Der Bauch, Die Bäuche | Abdomen |
| Der Bauchnabel, Die Bauchnabel | Navel |
| Der Bauer, Die Bauern; Die Bäuerin, Die Bäuerinnen | Farmer |
| Der Bauernhof, Die Bauernhöfe | Farm |
| Der Baum, Die Bäume | Tree |
| Der Beat | Beat music |
| Der Befreier, Die Befreier; Die Befreierin, Die Befreierinnen | Liberator |
| Der Begriff, Die Begriffe | Notion, Idea, Concept |

| German | English |
|---|---|
| Der Beidemeister, Die Beidemeistern; Die Beidemeisterin, Die Beidemeisterinnen | Lifeguard |
| Der Beistelltisch, Die Beistelltische | End Table |
| Der Beitrag, Die Beiträge | Contribution |
| Der Benutzer, Die Benutzer; Die Benutzerin, Die Benutzerinnen | User |
| Der Berater, Die Berater; Die Beaterin, Die Beaterinnen | Advisor |
| Der Bereich, Die Bereiche | Area (smaller) |
| Der Berg, Die Berge | Mountain |
| Der Bericht, Die Berichte | Report |
| Der Beruf, Die Berufe | Career |
| Der Beruf, Die Berufe | Occupation |
| Der Beruf, Die Berufe | Profession |
| Der Beschluss, Die Beschlüsse | Decision (group) |
| Der Beschuss | Shelling |
| Der Besen, Die Besen | Broom |
| Der Besuch, Die Besuche | Visit |
| Der Betrag, Die Beträge | Amount |
| Der Betreiber, Die Betreiber; Die Betreiberin, Die Betreiberinnen | Operator |
| Der Betrieb, Die Betriebe | Organization, Enterprise |
| Der Betriebshof, Die Betriebshöfe | Depot |
| Der Betrug, Die Betrüger | Fraud |
| Der Beutel, Die Taschen | Bag |
| Der Beweis, Die Beweise | Proof |
| Der Bewerber, Die Bewerber; Die Bewerberin, Die Bewerberinnen | Applicant |
| Der Bewerber, Die Bewerber; Die Bewerberin, Die Bewerberinnen | Candidate |
| Der Bewohner, Die Bewohner; Die Bewohnerin, Die Bewohnerinnen | Resident |
| Der Bezug, Die Bezüge | Reference |
| Der Bierdeckel, Die Bierdeckel | Coaster |
| Der Bildschirm, Die Bildschirme | Screen |
| Der Bischof, Die Bischöfe | Bishop |
| Der Bitcoin | Bitcoin |
| Der Bleistift, Die Bleistifte | Pencil (lead) |
| Der Blick, Die Blicke | View, Gaze, Look |
| Der Blinker, Die Blinker | Turn Signal |
| Der Blitz, Die Blitze | Lightning |
| Der Block, Die Blöcke | Block |
| Der Blumenkohl, Die Blumenkohle | Cauliflower |
| Der Blumenladen, Die Blumenladen | Flower Shop |

| German | English |
|---|---|
| Der Blutdruck, Die Blutdrücke | Blood Pressure |
| Der Boden, Die Böden | Bottom |
| Der Boden, Die Böden | Floor |
| Der Bonus, Die Bonus | Bonus |
| Der Bourbon, Die Bourbons | Bourbon |
| Der Bräutigam, Die Bräutigams | Bridegroom |
| Der Brief, Die Briefe | Letter |
| Der Briefkasten, Die Briefkästen | Mailbox |
| Der Brokkoli, Die Brokkolis | Broccoli |
| Der Bruder, Die Brüder | Brother |
| Der Bundesstaat, Die Bundesländer | German State |
| Der Bundestag | Parliament (Germany) |
| Der Bürger, Die Bürger; Die Bürgerin, Die Bürgerinnen | Citizen |
| Der Bürgersteig, Die Bürgersteige | Sidewalk |
| Der Bus, Die Busse | Bus |
| Der Büstenhalter, Die Büstenhalter (BH) | Bra |
| Der Champignon, Die Champignons | Mushroom (cooking) |
| Der Charakter, Die Charaktere | Character |
| Der Chef, Die Chefs; Die Chefin, Die Chefinnen | Boss |
| Der Chirug, Die Chirugen; Die Chirugerin, Die Chirugerinnen | Surgeon |
| Der Chor, Die Chöre | Choir |
| Der Christ, Die Christen; Die Christin, Die Christinnen | Christian |
| Der Cognac, Die Cognacs | Cognac |
| Der Cola-Automat, Die Cola-Automaten | Coke Machine, Soda Machine |
| Der Computer, Die Computer | Computer (electronic) |
| Der Couchtisch, Die Couchtische | Coffee Table |
| Der Cousin, Die Cousinen | Cousin |
| Der Dank | Thanks |
| Der Datensatz, Datensätze | Record |
| Der Daumen, Die Daumen | Thumb |
| Der Delphin, Die Delphine | Dolphin |
| Der Dezember | December |
| Der Diamant, Die Diamanten | Diamond |
| Der Dichter, Die Dichter | Poet |
| Der Dieb, Die Dieben; Die Diebin, Die Diebinnen | Thief |
| Der Dienst, Die Dienste | Service |
| Der Dienstag, Die Dienstage | Tuesday |
| Der Dividend, Die Dividenden | Dividend (fractions) |
| Der Doktor, Die Doktoren; Die Doktorin, Die Doktorinnen | Doctor, PhD |

| German | English |
| --- | --- |
| Der Dollar, Die Dollars | Dollar |
| Der Donner, Die Donner | Thunder |
| Der Donnerstag, Die Donnerstage | Thursday |
| Der Dorfdepp, Die Dorfdeppen | Village Idiot |
| Der Dorsch | Cod |
| Der Drachen, Die Drachen | Dragon |
| Der Drachen, Die Drachen | Kite |
| Der Drang, Die Dränge | Urge, Compulsion |
| Der Dreck | Dirt |
| Der Dritte | The Second |
| Der Druck | Pressure, Stress |
| Der Drucker, Die Drucker | Printer (machine) |
| Der Dschungel, Die Dschungel | Jungle |
| Der Dummkopf, Die Dummköpfe | Dumdum |
| Der Dünger, Die Dünger | Fertilizer |
| Der Dunst, Die Dünste | Mist, Haze |
| Der Ehemann, Die Ehemänner | Husband |
| Der Ehering, Die Eheringe | Wedding Ring |
| Der Einblick, Die Einblicke | Insight |
| Der Eindruck, Die Eindrücke | Impression |
| Der Eine, Die Einen | One |
| Der Eingriff, Die Eingriffe | Interference |
| Der Einkauf, Die Einkäufe | Purchase |
| Der Einklang, Die Einklänge | Harmony |
| Der Einsatz, Die Einsätze | Use, Input |
| Der Eintopf, Die Eintöpfe | Stew |
| Der Einunddreißigste | The Thirty-first |
| Der Einwohner, Die Einwohner; Die Einwohnerin, Die Einwohnerinnen | Residents |
| Der Einzelner, Die Einzelne; Die Einzelne, Die Einzelne | Individual |
| Der Einzug, Die Einzüge | Entry (into a place) |
| Der Elefant, Die Elefanten | Elephant |
| Der Elektriker, Die Elektriker; Die Elektrikerin, Die Elektrikerinnen | Electrician |
| Der Elektroherd, Die Elektroherde | Electric Stove |
| Der Elektronikladen, Die Elektronikladen | Electronics Store |
| Der Ellbogen, Die Ellenbogen | Elbow |
| Der Empfang, Die Empfänge | Reception, Radio |
| Der Erdboden, Die Erdböden; Die Erde, Die Erden | Soil |
| Der Erfolg, Die Erfolge | Success |
| Der Erlöser, Die Erlöser; Die Erlöserin, Die Erlöserinnen | Redeemer |

| German | English |
|---|---|
| Der Erreger, Die Erreger | Pathogen |
| Der Erretter, Die Erretter; Die Erretterin, Die Erretterinnen | Savior |
| Der Erste | The First |
| Der Ertrag, Die Erträge | Yield, Gain (agriculture) |
| Der Erzähler, Die Erzähler; Die Erzählerin, Die Erzählerinnen | Narrator |
| Der Erzbischof, Die Erzbischöfe | Archbishop |
| Der Esel, Die Esel | Donkey |
| Der Esslöffel, Die Esslöffeln | Tablespoon |
| Der Estragon | Tarragon |
| Der Euro, Die Euros | Euro |
| Der Ewachsene, Die Erwachsenen | Adult |
| Der Existenzialismus | Existentialism |
| Der Expressionismus | Expressionism |
| Der Expressionist, Die Expressionisten; Die Expressionistin, Die Expressionistinnen | Expressionist |
| Der Fachbereich, Die Fachbereiche | Department (university) |
| Der Fachleiter, Die Fachleiter; Die Fachleiterin, Die Fachleterinnen | Department Head (school) |
| Der Fahrer, Die Fahrer | Driver |
| Der Fahrersitz, Die Fahrersitze | Driver seat |
| Der Fahrgast, Die Fahrgäste | Passenger, Train, Taxi |
| Der Fahrkartenautomat, Die Fahrkartenautomaten | Ticket Vending Machine |
| Der Faktencheck, Die Faktenchecks | Fact Check |
| Der Fall, Die Fälle | Instance, Case, Event |
| Der Fallschirm, Die Falllschirme | Parachute |
| Der Fallschirmspringer, Die Fallschirmspringer; Die Fallschirmspringerin, Die Fallschirmspringerinnen | Parachutist |
| Der Fan, Die Fans | Fan (sports) |
| Der Fanatiker, Die Fanatiker; Die Fanatikerin, Die Fanatikerinnen | Zealot, Fanatic |
| Der Februar | February |
| Der Fehler, Die Fehler | Mistake |
| Der Feierabend, Die Feierabende | Quitting Time, End of Workday |
| Der Feiertag, Die Feiertagen | Holiday |
| Der Fels, Die Felsen | Rock |
| Der Feuerwehrmann, Die Feuerwehrmänner | Fireman |
| Der Film, Die Filme | Movie |
| Der Fing, Die Fänge | Catch (of the day) |
| Der Finger, Die Finger | Finger |
| Der Fingerhut, Die Fingerhüte | Thimble |

| German | English |
| --- | --- |
| Der Fisch, Die Fische | Fish |
| Der Fischgrätmuster, Die Fischgrätmuster | Herringbone Pattern |
| Der Fleck, Die Flecken | Spot |
| Der Fleck, Die Flecken | Stain |
| Der Flohmarkt, Die Flohmärkte | Flea Market |
| Der Flüchtling, Die Flüchtlinge | Refugee |
| Der Flug, Die Flüge | Flight |
| Der Flügel, Die Flügel | Wing |
| Der Flughafen, Die Flughäfen | Airport |
| Der Flugplatz, Die Flugplätze | Airfield |
| Der Flur, Die Flure | Hallway |
| Der Fluss, Die Flüsse | River |
| Der Forst, Die Forste | Forest |
| Der Fortschritt, Die Fortschritte | Progress, Advancement |
| Der Freak, Die Freaks | Freak |
| Der Freitag, Die Freitage | Friday |
| Der Fremde, Die Fremden | Stranger |
| Der Freund, Die Freunde | Friend |
| Der Frühling | Spring |
| Der Führerschein, Die Führerscheine | Driver's License |
| Der Fünfte | The Fifth |
| Der Funk | Radio (technical) |
| Der Fuß, Die Füße | Foot |
| Der Fußball, Die Fußbälle | Soccer |
| Der Fußgänger, Die Fußgänger; Die Fußgängerin, Die Fußgängerinnen | Pedestrian |
| Der Gang, Die Gänge | Aisle (also course as in three-course meal) |
| Der Gang, Die Gänge | Gear (car, bike) |
| Der Garten, Die Gärten | Garden |
| Der Gasherd, Die Gasherde | Gas Stove |
| Der Gast, Die Gäste | Guest |
| Der Geber, Die Geber; Die Geberin, Die Geberinnen | Giver |
| Der Gedanke, Die Gedanken | Thought |
| Der Gegenstand, Die Gegenstände | Item, Object, Article |
| Der Gegner, Die Gegner; Die Gegnerin, Die Gegnerinnen | Opponent |
| Der Geist, Die Geister | Ghost |
| Der Geist, Die Geister | Spirit |
| im Geiste | Spirit, in the |
| Der Geldautomat, Die Geldautomaten | ATM |
| Der Geldbeutel, Die Geldbeutel | Wallet |
| Der Geldschein, Die Geldscheine | Paper Cash, Bill |

| German | English |
|--------|---------|
| Der Genosse, Die Genossen; Die Genossin, Die Genossinnen | Companion, Comrade |
| Der Geruch, Die Gerüche | Smell |
| Der Geschäftsführer, Die Geschäftsführer; Die Geschäftsführerin, Die Geschäftsführerinnen | Manager, Business Director |
| Der Geschmack, Die Geschmäcke | Flavor |
| Der Gewinn, Die Gewinne | Profit |
| Der Gewinner, Die Gewinner; Die Gewinnerin, Die Gewinnernnen | Winner |
| Der Gin, Die Gins | Gin |
| Der Gipfel, Die Gipfel | Peak, Summit |
| Der Glamour | Glamor |
| Der Glanz | Polish |
| Der Glanz | Shine, Sheen |
| Der Glaube, Die Glauben | Belief |
| Der Gläubige, Die Gläubigen | Believer |
| Der Gliederflüßler, Die Gliederflüßler | Arthropod (shrimp, crabs, lobsters) |
| Der Globalizierung | Globalization |
| Der Golf, Die Gölfe | Gulf |
| Der Gorilla, Die Gorillas | Gorilla |
| Der Gott, Die Götter | God |
| Der Grad, Die Grade | Grade (military, weather, math) |
| Der Grill, Die Grills | Barbecue Grill |
| Der Großhändler, Die Großhändler; Die Großhändlerin, Die Großhändlerinnen | Wholesaler |
| Der Großraum, Die Großräume | Metro Area |
| Der Großvater, Die Großväter | Grandfather |
| Der Grund, Die Gründe | Reason |
| Der Gürtel, Die Gurtel | Belt |
| Der Hagel | Hail |
| Der Hahn, Die Hähne | Rooster |
| Der Hai, Die Haie | Shark |
| Der Halbleiter, Die Halbleiter | Semi-conductor |
| Der Hals, Die Hälse | Neck |
| Der Hammerhai, Die Hammerhaie | Shark, Hammerhead |
| Der Hamster, Die Hamster | Hamster |
| Der Handel | Trade, Deal (economic) |
| Der Handmixer, Die Handmixer | Mixer |
| Der Hanschuh, Die Handschuhe | Glove |
| Der Hase, Die Hasen | Rabbit |
| Der Haushalt, Die Haushalte | Household |
| Der Heilbutt | Halibut |

| German | English |
|---|---|
| Der Heilige, Die Heiligen | Saint |
| Der Heizofen, Die Heizöfen | Furnace |
| Der Hemmschuh, Die Hemmschuhe | Stumbling Block |
| Der Hengst, Die Hengste | Stallion |
| Der Herausgeber, Die Herausgeber; Die Herausgeberin, Die Herausgeberinnen | Publisher |
| Der Herbst, Die Herbste | Autumn |
| Der Herd, Die Herde | Stove |
| Der Hering | Herring |
| Der Herr, Die Herren | Gentleman, Lord |
| Der Herr, Die Herren | Lord |
| Der Hersteller, Die Hersteller | Manufacturer |
| Der Himmel, Der Himmel | Sky, Heaven |
| Der Hinduismus | Hinduism |
| Der Hintergrund, Die Hintergründe | Background |
| Der Hinweis, Die Hinweise | Hint |
| Der Hirte, Die Hirten; Die Hirterin, Die Hirterinnen | Herdsman |
| Der Hof, Die Höfe | Yard |
| Der Honig, Die Honige | Honey |
| Der Hosenanzug, Die Hosenanzüge | Pantsuit |
| Der Hubschrauber, Die Hubschrauber | Helicopter |
| Der Hügel, Die Hügel | Hill |
| Der Hummer, Die Hummer | Lobster |
| Der Hund, Die Hunde | Dog |
| Der Husten | Cough |
| Der Hut, Die Hüte | Hat |
| Der Hüter, Die Hüter; Die Hüterin, Die Hüterinnen | Guardian |
| Der Idiot, Die Idioten; Die Idiotin, Die Idiotinnen | Idiot |
| Der Impressionismus | Impressionism |
| Der Impressionist, Die Impressionisten; Die Impressionistin, Die Impressionistinnen | Impressionist |
| Der Inspektor, Die Inspektoren; Die Inspektorin, Die Inspektorinnen | Inspector |
| Der Irak | Iraq |
| Der Iran | Iran |
| Der Irrtum, Die Irrtümer | Error |
| Der Januar | January |
| Der Jemen | Yemen |
| Der Job, Die Jobs | Job |
| Der Juli | July |
| Der Junge, Die Jungen | Young Man, Boy |
| Der Junggeselle, Die Junggesellen | Bachelor |

| German | English |
|---|---|
| Der Juni | June |
| Der Kabeljau | Cod |
| Der Käfer, Die Käfer | Beetle |
| Der Kaffee, Die Kaffee | Coffee |
| Der Kaffeeautomat, Die Kaffeeutomaten | Coffee Vending Machine |
| Der Kamerad, Die Kameraden; Die Kameradin, Die Kameradinnen | Comrade |
| Der Kamin, Die Kamine | Fireplace |
| Der Kampf, Die Kämpfe | Struggle |
| Der Kandidat, Die Kandidaten; Die Kandidatin, Die Kandidatinnen | Candidate |
| Der Kapitän, Die Kapitäne, Die Kapitänin, Die Kapitäninnen | Captain |
| Der Kardinal, Die Kardinäle | Cardinal |
| Der Kasten, Die Kästen | Box, Chest |
| Der Käufer, Die Käufer; Die Käuferin, Die Käuferinnen | Buyer |
| Der Kerl, Die Kerle | Guy |
| Der Ketchup, Die Ketchudps | Ketchup |
| Der Kichererbsen, Die Kichererbsen | Chickpea |
| Der Klang | Sound (harmonies) |
| Der Klassenkamerad, Die Klassenkameraden; Die Klassenkameradin, Die Klassenkameradinnen | Classmate |
| Der Klassenkampf, Die Klassenkämpfe | Class Struggle |
| Der Klassenkrieg, Die Klassenkriege | Class Warfare |
| Der Klebstoff, Die Klebstoffe | Adhesive, Glue |
| Der Klempner, Die Klempner | Plumber |
| Der Klimaschutz | Climate Protection |
| Der Klub, Die Klubs | Club |
| Der Knabe, Die Knaben | Boy |
| Der Knacker, Die Knacker | Cracker |
| Der Knoblauch | Garlic |
| Der Knöchel, Die Knöchel | Ankle |
| Der Knochen, Die Knochen | Bone |
| Der Knopf, Die Knöpfe | Button |
| Der Koffer, Die Koffer | Suitcase |
| Der Kofferraum, Die Kofferräume | Car Trunk |
| Der Kollege, Die Kollegen | Colleague |
| Der Kommandant, Die Kommandanten | Commander |
| Der Komminismus | Communism |
| Der Kommunist, Die Kommunisten; Die Kommunistin, Die Kommunistinnen | Communist |
| Der Kongo | Republic of the Congo |
| Der Kongress, Die Kongresse | Congress |

| German | English |
|---|---|
| Der König, Die Könige | King |
| Der Kopf, Die Köpfe | Head |
| Der Kopfball, Die Kopfbälle | Header (soccer) |
| Der Kopfjäger, Die Kopfjäger; Die Kopfjägerin, Die Kopfjägerinnen | Headhunter |
| Der Kopfsalat (also Der Salat), Die Kopfsalate | Lettuce Head |
| Der Korbball, Die Korbbälle | Basketball |
| Der Koriander | Cilantro |
| Der Körper, Die Körper | Body |
| Der Krall, Die Krallen | Claw, Hook (as in hand) |
| Der Krankenpfleger, Die Krankenpflegerin | Nurse, male |
| Der Krankenwagen, Die Krankenwagen | Ambulance |
| Der Krebs, Die Krebse | Cancer |
| Der Krebs, Die Krebse (Some *Krebse* are not crabs.) | Crab (classification) |
| Der Kreis, Die Kreise | Circle |
| Der Kreuzfahrtschiff, Die Kreuzfahrtschiffe | Cruise Ship |
| Der Krieg, Die Kriege | War |
| Der Kubismus | Cubism |
| Der Kubist, Die Kubisten; Die Kubistin, Die Kubistinnen | Cubist |
| Der Kugelschreiber, Die Kugelschreiber | Pen (ballpoint) |
| Der Kühlschrank, Die Kühlschränke | Refrigerator |
| Der Kuli, Die Kulis | Pen (ballpoint) |
| Der Kunde, Die Kunden | Customer |
| Der Kundendienst, Die Kundendienste | Customer Service |
| Der Kunststoff, Die Kunststoff | Plastic |
| Der Kurs, Die Kurse | Course |
| Der Kurzzeitwecker, Die Kurzzeitwecker | Timer |
| Der Lachs, Die Lachse | Salmon |
| Der Laden, Die Laden | Store, Shop |
| Der Landsitz, Die Landsitze | Manor, Country Estate |
| Der Laptop, Die Laptops | Laptop |
| Der Lärm | Noise |
| Der Lastkraftwagen (Lkw), Die Lastkraftwagen | Truck |
| Der Lebenslauf, Die Lebensläufe | Resume, CV |
| Der Lehrer, Die Lehrer; Die Lehrerin, Die Lehrerinnen | Teacher |
| Der Leiter, Die Leiter; Die Leiterin, Die Leiterinnen | Leader, Director |
| Der Libanon | Lebanon |
| Der Lidschatten, Die Lidschatten | Eye Shadow |
| Der Lippenstift, Die Lippenstifte | Lipstick |
| Der Löffel, Die Löffel | Spoon |

| German | English |
|--------|---------|
| Der Lohn, Die Löhne | Wage |
| Der Löwe, Die Löwen | Leo |
| Der Löwe, Die Löwen; Die Löwin, Die Löwinnen | Lion |
| Der Magen, Die Mägen | Stomach |
| Der Magnat, Die Magnaten; Die Magnatin, Die Magnatinnen | Magnate |
| Der Mai | May |
| Der Mais | Corn |
| Der Mann, Die Männer | Husband |
| Der Mann, Die Männer | Man |
| Der Mantel, Die Mäntel | Coat |
| Der Marathon, Die Marathons | Marathon |
| Der Markt, Die Märkte | Market |
| Der März | March |
| Der Maus, Die Mäuse | Mouse |
| Der Meister, Die Meister | Master |
| Der Mensch, Die Menschen | Human |
| Der Messbecher, Die Messbecher | Measuring Cup |
| Der Messlöffel, Die Messlöffeln | Measuring Spoon |
| Der Mietwagen, Die Mietwagen | Rental Car |
| Der Minimalismus | Minimalism |
| Der Minimalist, Die Minimalisten; Die Minimalistin, Die Minimalistinnen | Minimalist |
| Der Minut, Die Minuten | Minute |
| Der Misserfolg, Die Misserfolge | Failure |
| Der Mitarbeiter, Die Mitarbeiter; Die Mitarbeiterin, Die Mitarbeiterinnen | Co-worker (worker in a group) |
| Der Mitbewerber, Die Mitbewerber; Die Mitbewerberin, Die Mitbewerberinnen | Competitor |
| Der Mitbewohner, Die Mitbewohner; Die Mitbewohnerin, Die Mitbewohnerinnen | Roommate |
| Der Mittag, Die Mittage | Noon |
| Der Mittäter, Die Mittäter; Die Mittäterin, Die Mittäterinnen | Accomplice |
| Der Mittwoch, Die Mittwochen | Wednesday |
| Der Moment, Die Momente | Moment |
| Der Monat, Die Monate | Month |
| Der Mond, Die Monde | Moon |
| Der Montag, Die Montage | Monday |
| Der Morgen, Die Morgen | Morning |
| Der Moskito, Die Moskitos (also Die Stechmücke) | Mosquito |
| Der Motor, Die Motoren | Engine |
| Der Müll | Trash |
| Der Mund, Die Münder | Mouth |

| German | English |
|---|---|
| Der Muslim, Die Muslime | Muslim |
| Der Nachbar, Die Nachbarn | Neighbor |
| Der Nachlass, Die Nachlässe | Estate, Inheritance |
| Der Nachmittag, Die Nachmittage | Afternoon |
| Der Nagellack, Die Nagellacke | Nail Polish |
| Der Name, Die Namen | Name |
| Der Narr, Die Narren; Die Närrin, Die Närrinnen | Fool |
| Der Nationalist, Die Nationalisten | Nationalist |
| Der Nebel, Die Nebel | Fog |
| Der Neffe, Die Neffen | Nephew |
| Der Niedergang | Decline |
| Der Nihilismus | Nihilism |
| Der Nihilist, Die Nihilisten; Die Nihilistin, Die Nihilistinnen | Nihilist |
| Der Norden | North |
| Der Notfall, Die Notfälle | Emergency |
| Der November | November |
| Der Nussknacker, Die Nussknacker | Nutcracker |
| Der Nutzen, Die Nutzen | Benefit |
| Der Offizier, Die Offiziere; Die Offizierin, Die Offizierinnen | Officer |
| Der Ohrring, Die Ohrringe | Earring |
| Der Oktober | October |
| Der Oktopus, Die Oktopusse | Octopus |
| Der Öltanker, Die Öltanker | Oil Tanker |
| Der Oman | Oman |
| Der Onkel, Die Onkel | Uncle |
| Der Optimismus | Optimism |
| Der Optimist, Die Optimisten; Die Optimistin, Die Optimistinnen | Optimist |
| Der Orangensaft, Die Orangensafte | Orange Juice |
| Der Ordner, Die Ordner | Folder (file) |
| Der Ort, Die Orte | Place |
| Der Osten | East |
| Der Papa, Die Papas | Dad |
| Der Papagei, Die Papageien | Parrot |
| Der Papst, Die Päpste | Pope |
| Der Park, Die Parks | Park |
| Der Partner, Die Partner; Die Partnerin, Die Partnerinnen | Partner (mate) |
| Der Passagier, Die Passagiere; Die Passagierin, Die Passagierinnen | Passenger, Aviation, Nautical |
| Der Pazifik | Pacific |

| German | English |
|---|---|
| Der Pazifist, Die Pazifisten; Die Pazifistin, Die Pazifistinnen | Pacifist |
| Der Pfad, Die Pfade | Path |
| Der Pfannenwender (or Der Wender), Die Pfannenwender | Spatula |
| Der Pfarrer, Die Pfarrer; Die Pfarrerin, Die Pfarrerinnen | Pastor |
| Der Pfarrer, Die Pfarrer; Die Pfarrerin, Die Pfarrerinnen | Priest |
| Der Pfirsich, Die Pfirsiche | Peach |
| Der Pfleger, Die Pfleger; Die Pflegerin, Die Pflegerinnen | Caregiver |
| Der Pfosten, Die Pfosten | Goal Post |
| Der Physiotherapeut, Die Physiotherapeuten; Die Physiotherapeutin, Die Physiotherapeutinnen | Physical Therapist |
| Der Pilot, Die Piloten; Die Politin, Die Pilotinnen | Pilot |
| Der Pilz, Die Pilze | Mushroom (fungus) |
| Der Pirat, Die Piraten; Die Piratin, Die Piratinnen | Pirate |
| Der Plan, Die Pläne | Plan |
| Der Planet, Die Planeten | Planet |
| Der Platz, Die Plätze | Place |
| Der Pokal, Die Pokale | Trophy Cup |
| Der Politiker, Die Politiker; Die Politikerin, Die Politikerinnen | Politician |
| Der Präsident, Die Präsidenten | President |
| Der Prophet, Die Propheten; Die Prophetin, Die Prophetinnen | Prophet |
| Der Prozess, Die Prozesse | Trial |
| Der Pterodactylus, Die Pterodactylen | Pterodactyl |
| Der Puderzucker | Powdered Sugar |
| Der Pulli, Die Pullis | Sweater |
| Der Punkt, Die Punkte | Point |
| Der Rabatt, Die Rabatte | Discount (rebate) |
| Der Radfahrer, Die Radfahrer; Die Radfahrerin, Die Radfahrerinnen | Cyclist |
| Der Radioempfänger, Die Radioempfänger | Radio (receiver) |
| Der Rahmen, Die Rahmen | Frame |
| Der Rand, Die Ränder | Edge, Boundary |
| Der Rasenmäher, Die Rasenmäher | Lawn Mower |
| Der Rat, Die Räte | Council, Guidance |
| Der Räuber, Die Räuber; Die Räuberin, Die Räuberinnen | Robber |
| Der Rauch | Smoke |
| Der Raum, Die Räume | Space (astronomy) |

| German | English |
|---|---|
| Der Rechner, Die Rechner | Calculator |
| Der Rechner, Die Rechner | Computer (someone or something that computes) |
| Der Redakteur, Die Redakteure; Die Redakteurin, Die Redakteurinnen | Editor |
| Der Regen, Die Regenzeit | Rain |
| Der Regenmantel, Die Regenmäntel | Raincoat |
| Der Regenschirm, Die Regenschirme | Umbrella |
| Der Reichtum, Die Reichtümer | Wealth |
| Der Reifen, Die Reifen | Tire |
| Der Reis | Rice |
| Der Reisende, Die Reisenden; Die Reisende, Die Reisenden | Traveler |
| Der Reisepass, Die Reisepässe | Passport |
| Der Reißverschluss, Die Reißverschlüsse | Zipper |
| Der Retter, Die Retter; Die Retterin, Die Reteterinnen | Rescuer |
| Der Rettungsschwimmer, Die Rettungsschwimmer; Die Rettungsschwimmerin, Die Rettungsschwimmerinnen | Lifeguard |
| Der Richter, Die Richter; Die Richterin, Die Richterinnen | Judge |
| Der Ring, Die Ringe | Ring |
| Der Rock, Die Röcke | Skirt |
| Der Roggen | Rye |
| Der Roman, Die Romane | Novel |
| Der Romantiker, Die Romantiker; Die Romantikerin, Die Romantikerinnen | Romantic |
| Der Römersalat, Die Römersalate | Lettuce, Romaine |
| Der Rotwein, Die Rotweine | Red Wine |
| Der Rücken, Die Rücken | Back |
| Der Rücksitz, Die Rücksitze | Backseat |
| Der Ruhestand | Retirement |
| Der Rum, Die Rums | Rum |
| Der Rye, Der Roggenwhisky, Die Roggenwhiskys | Rye Whiskey |
| Der Sadismus | Sadism |
| Der Sadist, Die Sadisten; Die Sadistin, Die Sadistinnen | Sadist |
| Der Saft, Die Säfte | Juice |
| Der Salat, Die Salate | Lettuce |
| Der Salat, Die Salate | Salad |
| Der Samstag, Die Samstage | Saturday |
| Der Sand, Der Sand | Sand |

| German | English |
| --- | --- |
| Der Sang, Die Sänge | Song |
| Der Sänger, Die Sänger; Die Sängerin, Die Sängerinnen | Singer |
| Der Satz, Die Sätze | Sentence |
| Der Schaden, Die Schäden | Damage |
| Der Schäfer, Die Schäfer; Die Schäferin, Die Schäferinnen | Shepheard |
| Der Schal, Die Schals | Scarf |
| Der Schatten, Die Schatten | Shadow |
| Der Schauspieler, Die Schauspieler; Die Schauspielerin, Die Schauspielerinnen | Actor, Actress |
| Der Scheck, Die Schecks | Check |
| Der Scheibenwischer, Die Scheibenwischer | Windshield Wiper |
| Der Scheinwerfer, Die Scheinwerfer | Headlight |
| Der Schild, Die Schilde (different from Das Schild) | Shield (that a warrior carries) |
| Der Schlaf | Sleep |
| Der Schlamm | Mud |
| Der Schlittschuh, Die Schlittschuhe | Ice Skate |
| Der Schlüssel, Die Schlüssel | Key |
| Der Schmerz, Die Schmerzen | Pain (bodily) |
| Der Schmuck, Die Schmucken | Jewelry |
| Der Schmuckladen, Die Schmuckläden | Jewelry Store |
| Der Schmutz | Dirt |
| Der Schnabel, Die Schnäbel | Beak, birds |
| Der Schnaps | Schnaps |
| Der Schnee | Snow |
| Der Schneebesen, Die Schneebesen | Whisk |
| Der Schnitt, Die Schnitte | Cut (textile, film) |
| Der Schnürsenkel, Die Schnürsenkel | Shoelace |
| Der Schock, Die Schocks | Shock |
| Der Schöpfer, Die Schöpfer; Die Schöpferin, Die Schöpferinnen | Creator |
| Der Schöplöffel, Die Löffel | Ladle |
| Der Schoß, Die Schöße | Lap |
| Der Schrecken, Die Schrecken | Horror, Fright |
| Der Schreibtisch, Die Schreibtische | Desk |
| Der Schritt, Die Schritte | Step |
| Der Schube, Die Schübe | Thrust, Boost |
| Der Schuh, Die Schuhe | Shoe |
| Der Schuhladen, Die Schuhladen | Shoe Store |
| Der Schulbus, Die Schulbusse | School Bus |
| Der Schüler, Die Studenten | Student |

| German | English |
|---|---|
| Der Schuss, Die Schüsse | Shot (gun shot or shot on goal) |
| Der Schutz | Protection, Shelter, Conservation |
| Der Schütze, Die Schützen | Sagittarius |
| Der Schwamm, Die Schwämme | Sponge |
| Der Schwarm, Die Schwärme | Flock |
| Der Schwerpunkt, Die Schwerpunkte | Focus, Main Point |
| Der Schwertfisch | Swordfish |
| Der Schwiegervater, Die Schwiegerväter | Father-in-law |
| Der Scotch, Die Scotchs | Scotch |
| Der Sechste | The Sixth |
| Der See, Die Seen | Lake |
| Der Segen, Die Segen (plural is rare) | Blessing |
| Der Sekretär, Die Sekretäre; Die Sekretärin, Die Sekretärinnen | Secretary |
| Der Sellerie, Die Sellerie | Celery |
| Der Senat, Die Senate | Senate |
| Der Senator, Die Senatoren; Die Senatorin, Die Senatorinnen | Senator |
| Der Senf, Die Senfe | Mustard |
| Der September | September |
| Der Sessel, Die Sessel | Armchair |
| Der Siebente | The Seventh |
| Der Sieg, Die Siege | Victory |
| Der Sinn, Die Sinne | Mind, Sense |
| Der Sitzplatz, Die Sitzplätze | Seat |
| Der Skorpion, Die Skorpione | Scorpio |
| Der Sohn, Die Söhne | Son |
| Der Soldat, Die Soldaten | Soldier |
| Der Sommer, Die Sommer | Summer |
| Der Sonnabend, Die Sonnabende | Saturday |
| Der Sonnenaufgang, Die Sonnenaufgänge | Sunrise |
| Der Sonnenuntergang, Die Sonnenuntergänge | Sunset |
| Der Sonntag, Die Sonntage | Sunday |
| Der Sopranist, Die Sopranisten; Die Sopranistin, Die Sopranistinnen | Soprano |
| Der Spaß, Die Späße | Fun |
| Der Spaziergang, Die Spaziergänge | Walk |
| Der Speck | Bacon |
| Der Speicher, Die Speicher | Storage (memory, attic) |
| Der Speicherplatz, Die Speicherplätze | Computer Storage |
| Der Spiegel, Die Spiegel | Mirror |

| German | English |
|---|---|
| Der Spion, Die Spione; Die Spionin, Die Spioninnen | Spy |
| Der Sport | Athletics |
| Der Sportplatz, Die Sportplätze | Athletic Field, Arena |
| Der Sportschuh, Die Sportschuhe | Athletic Shoe |
| Der Sprengstoff, Die Sprengstoffe | Explosive Substance |
| Der Staat, Die Staaten | State (Bavaria, Florida, etc.) |
| Der Staatsanwalt, Die Staatsanwälte; Die Staatsanwältin, Die Staatsanwältinnen | State Attorney |
| Der Staatspräsident, Die Staatspräsidenten; Die Staatspräsidentin, Die Staatspräsidentinnen | State President, Governor |
| Der Stachel, Die Stacheln | Thorn |
| Der Standort, Die Standorte | Location (fixed) |
| Der Staub, Die Stäube | Dust |
| Der Stein, Die Steine | Stone |
| Der Steinbock, Die Steinböcke | Capricorn |
| Der Stern, Die Sterne | Star |
| Der Stich, Die Stiche | Sting, Prick, Stab |
| Der Stiefel, Die Stiefel | Boot (shoe) |
| Der Stiefsohn, Die Stiefsöhne | Stepson |
| Der Stier, Die Stiere | Taurus |
| Der Stift, Die Stifte | Writing Utensil (any type) |
| Der Stock, Die Stock | Floor, Story (building) |
| Der Stoff, Die Stoffe | Fabric |
| Der Strafstoß, Die Strafstöße | Penalty (sport) |
| Der Strahl, Die Strahlen | Ray |
| Der Strand, Die Strände | Beach |
| Der Strass, Die Strasse | Rhinestone |
| Der Streich, Die Streiche | Coup |
| Der Streik, Die Streike | Strike, Walkout |
| Der Streit, Die Streite | Dispute |
| Der Stress | Stress |
| Der Strom, Die Ströme | Current (electricity) |
| Der Studienberater, Die Studienberater; Die Studienberatin, Die Studienberatinnen | Academic Advisor |
| Der Stuhl, Die Stühle | Chair |
| Der Sturm und Drang | Sturm und Drang/Storm and Stress (German literary movement, 18th Century) |
| Der Sturm, Die Stürme | Storm |
| Der Sturm, Die Stürme | Windstorm |
| Der Sudan | Sudan |
| Der Süden, Die Souths | South |
| Der Supermarkt, Die Supermärkte | Supermarket |

| German | English |
| --- | --- |
| Der Tag, Die Tagen | Day (entire) |
| Der Tanz, Die Tänze | Dance |
| Der Taschenrechner, Die Taschenrechner | Pocket Calculator |
| Der Taugenichts, Die Taugenichtse | Good-for-Nothing (as in the memoirs of von Eichendorff) |
| Der Taxifahrer, Die Taxifahrer; Die Taxifahrerin, Die Taxifahrerinnen | Taxi Driver |
| Der Tee, Die Tees | Tea |
| Der Teelöffel, Die Teelöffeln | Teaspoon |
| Der Teich, Die Teiche | Pond |
| Der Teig, Die Teige | Dough |
| Der Teil, Die Teile | Part |
| Der Teller, Die Teller | Plate |
| Der Tenor, Die Tenöre | Tenor |
| Der Terroranschlag, Die Terroränschlage | Terrorist Attack |
| Der Terrorismus | Terrorism |
| Der Terrorist, Die Terroristen; Die Terroristin, Die Terroristinnen | Terrorist |
| Der Thunfisch, Die Thunfische | Tuna |
| Der Tiergarten, Die Tiergärten | Zoo |
| Der Tierkreis, Die Tierkreise | Zodiac |
| Der Tierpark, Die Tierparks | Zoo |
| Der Tierschützer, Die Tierschützer; Die Tierschützerin, Die Tierschützerinnen | Animal Rights Activist |
| Der Tiger, Die Tiger | Tiger |
| Der Tintenfisch | Squid |
| Der Tisch, Die Tische | Table |
| Der Titel, Die Titel | Title (book, film) |
| Der Tod, Die Tode | Death |
| Der Todesfall, Die Todesfälle | Death |
| Der Ton, Die Töne | Tone (sine wave) |
| Der Topf, Die Töpfe | Pot (metal) |
| Der Tornado, Die Tornados | Tornado |
| Der Torwart, Die Torwarte; Die Torwartin, Die Torwartinnen | Goalie |
| Der Trainer, Die Trainer; Die Trainerin, Die Trainerinnen | Coach (sports) |
| Der Traubensaft, Die Traubensäfte | Grape Juice |
| Der Traum, Die Träume | Dream |
| Der Trinkhalm, Die Trinkhalme | Drinking Straw |
| Der Türgriff, Die Türgriffe | Doorhandle |
| Der Türknauf, Die Türknäufe | Doorknob |
| Der Turnschuh, Die Turnschuhe | Sneaker |

| German | English |
|---|---|
| Der Turnschuh, Die Turnschuhe (usually plural) | Gym Shoe |
| Der Tycoon, Die Tycoons | Tycoon |
| Der Typ, Die Typen | Type (colloquially a fellow, guy) |
| Der Umhang, Die Umhänge | Cloak |
| Der Umsatz, Die Umsätze | Sales, Turnover |
| Der Untergang, Die Untergänge | Fall, Collapse |
| Der Unterschied, Die Unterschiede | Difference |
| Der Unterstützer, Die Unterstützer; Die Unterstützerin, Die Unterstützerinnen | Supporter, Endorser |
| Der Untertitel, Die Untertitel | Subtitle |
| Der Ureinwohner, Die Ureinwohner; Die Ureinwohnerin, Die Ureinwohnerinnen | Native |
| Der Urlaub, Die Urlaube (plural is rare) | Vacation |
| Der Ursprung, Die Ursprünge | Origin |
| Der US-Bundesstaat, Die US-Bundesstaaten | State (within the US) |
| Der Vater, Die Väter | Father |
| Der Vatikan | Vatican City |
| Der Verbraucher, Die Verbraucher; Die Verbraucherin, Die Verbraucherinnen | Consumer |
| Der Verbrecher, Die Verbrecher; Die Verbrecherin, Die Verbrecherinnen | Criminal |
| Der Verdächtige, Die Verdächtigen; Die Verdächtige, Die Verdächtigen | Suspect |
| Der Verein, Die Vereine | Association (club) |
| Der Verfall | Deterioration, Decay |
| Der Verkäufer, Die Verkäufer; Die Verkäuferin, Die Verkäuferinnen | Seller |
| Der Verlobungring, Die Verlobungringe | Engagement Ring |
| Der Verlust, Die Verluste | Loss |
| Der Verrat | Betrayal, Treason |
| Der Versicherer, Die Versicherer | Insurer |
| Der Verstärker, Die Verstärker | Amplifier |
| Der Vertrag, Die Verträge | Contract |
| Der Vertreter, Die Vertreterin | Agent, Representative |
| Der Verwandte, Die Verwandten | Relative (family, next of kin) |
| Der Verzicht, Die Verzichte | Disclaimer |
| Der Vierte | The Fourth |
| Der Vogel, Die Vögel | Bird |
| Der Vorfahre, Die Vorfahren | Ancestor |
| Der Vorgesetzter, Die Vorgesetzten; Die Vorgesetzte, Die Vorgesetzten | Supervisor |
| Der Vorhang, Die Vorhänge | Curtain (not thin) |
| Der Vorname, Die Vornamen | Name, First |

| German | English |
|---|---|
| Der Vorrat, Die Vorräte | Inventory, Supply |
| Der Vorrat, Die Vorräte | Supply, Inventory |
| Der Vorschlag, Die Vorschläge | Proposal, Suggestion |
| Der Vorsitzende, Die Vorsitzenden; Die Vorsitzende, Die Vorsitzenden | Chairperson |
| Der Vorteil, Die Vorteile | Advantage |
| Der Vortrag, Die Vorträge | Lecture, Presentation |
| Der Vorwurf, Die Vorwürfe | Allegations |
| Der Wächter, Die Wächter; Die Wächterin, Die Wächterinnen | Guard |
| Der Wähler, Die Wähler; Die Wählerin, Die Wählerinnen | Voter |
| Der Wahlkampf, Die Wahlkämpfe | Election Campaign |
| Der Wald, Die Wälder | Wood, tree grouping |
| Der Waldbrand, Die Waldbrände | Forest Fire |
| Der Wallach, Die Wallache | Gelding |
| Der Waschlappen, Die Waschlappen | Washcloth |
| Der Wassermann, Die Wassermänner | Aquarius |
| Der Wechsel, Die Wechsel | Change (in weather, etc.) |
| Der Wecker, Die Wecker | Alarm Clock |
| Der Weg, Die Wege | Path, Way |
| Der Weg, Die Wege | Way |
| Der Wein, Die Weine | Wine |
| Der Weiße Hai, Die weißen Haie | Great White Shark |
| Der Weißwein, Die Weißweine | White Wine |
| Der Weizen | Wheat |
| Der Welpe, Die Welpen | Puppy |
| Der Werktag, Die Werktagen | Workday |
| Der Werkzeug, Die Werkzeuge | Tool |
| Der Wert, Die Werte | Value |
| Der Westen | West |
| Der Wettbewerb, Die Wettbewerbe | Competition |
| Der Whisky, Die Whiskys | Whiskey |
| Der Widder, Die Widder | Aries |
| Der Widerstand, Die Widerstände | Resistance |
| Der Will, Die Willen | Determination |
| Der Wille, Die Willen | Will (inner commitment) |
| Der Wind, Die Winde | Wind |
| Der Windstoß, Die Windstöße | Gust |
| Der Winkel, Die Winkel | Angle |
| Der Winter, Die Winter | Winter |
| Der Witwer, Die Witwer | Widower |
| Der Witz, Die Witze | Joke |
| Der Wodka, Die Wodkas | Vodka |

| German | English |
| --- | --- |
| Der Wolkenkratzer, Die Wolkenkratzer | Skyscraper |
| Der Wortschatz, Die Wortschätze | Vocabulary |
| Der Würfel, Die Würfel | Cube, Dice |
| Der Yankee, Die Yankees | Yankee |
| Der Zähler, Die Zähler; Die Zählerin, Die Zählerinnen | Counter (person who counts) |
| Der Zahn, Die Tooths | Tooth |
| Der Zahnartzt, Die Zahnärtzten, Die Zahnärtztin, Die Zahnärtztinnen | Dentist |
| Der Zahnschmerz, Die Zahnschmerzen | Toothache |
| Der Zebrastreifen, Die Zebrastreifen | Crosswalk |
| Der Zeigefinger, Die Zeigefinger | Index Finger |
| Der Ziegenbock, Die Ziegenböcke | Goat, Billy |
| Der Zigarrettenautomat, Die Zigarrettenautomaten | Cigarette Machine |
| Der Zimt | Cinnamon |
| Der Zins, Die Zinsen | Interest (on money) |
| Der Zirkus, Die Zirkusse | Circus |
| Der Zoll, Die Zölle | Tariff, Customs, Levy, Toll |
| Der Zoo, Die Zoos | Zoo |
| Der Zooladen, Die Zooladen | Pet Store |
| Der Zorn | Anger |
| Der Zucker | Sugar |
| Der Zuckerwürfel, Die Zuckerwürfel | Sugar Cube |
| Der Zufall, Die Zufälle | Coincidence, Chance |
| Der Zug, Die Züge | Train |
| Der Zuhörer, Die Zuhörer; Die Zuhörerin, Die Zuhörerinnen | Listener |
| Der Zusammenhang, Die Zusammenhänge | Context |
| Der Zustand, Die Zustände | Condition (appearance) |
| Der Zweck, Die Zwecke | Purpose, Function |
| Der Zweig, Die Zweige | Twig (tree) |
| Der Zweite, Die Zweiten | Second |
| Der Zwiebel, Die Zwiebeln | Onion |
| Der Zwilling, Die Zwillinge | Gemini |
| Der Zwilling, Die Zwillinge | Twin |

# FEMININE (*DIE*) NOUNS

| German | English |
|---|---|
| Die Abfahrt, Die Abfahrten | Departure (vehicle, train) |
| Die Abgabe, Die Abgaben | Deadline, Delivery, Levy |
| Die Abhängung, Die Abhängungen | Suspension |
| Die Abkündigung, Die Abkündigungen | Discontinuation |
| Die Ablehnung, Die Ablehnungen | Rejection |
| Die Abreise, Die Abreisen | Departure (for a trip) |
| Die Absicht, Die Absichten | Intention |
| Die Abstimmung, Die Abstimmungen | Vote (choosing a direction, process) |
| Die Abtei, Die Abteien | Abbey |
| Die Abteilung, Die Abteilungen | Department |
| Die Abtreibung, Die Abtreibungen | Abortion |
| Die Abwehr | Defense (sport), Resistance (as in WWII) |
| Die Acrylfarbe, Die Acrylfarben | Acrylic Paint |
| Die Adresse, Die Adressen | Address |
| Die Affe, Die Affen, Die Äffin, Die Äffinnen | Monkey |
| Die Agentur, Die Agenturen | Agency |
| Die Aktienoption, Die Aktienoptionen | Stock Option |
| Die Aktion, Die Aktionen | Action |
| Die Aktivität, Die Aktivitäten | Activity |
| Die Algebra, Die Algeberen | Algebra |
| Die Alpen | Alps |
| Die Ameise, Die Ameisen | Ant |
| Die Ampel, Die Ampeln | Stoplight, Traffic Light |
| Die Amtseinführung, Die Amtseinführungen | Inauguration (Office, Presidential) |
| Die Amtszeit, Die Amtszeiten | Term (in office) |
| Die Ananas, Die Ananas | Pineapple |
| Die Anatomie, Die Anatomien | Anatomy |
| Die Anderen, Die Anderen | Others |
| Die Anerkennung, Die Anerkennungen | Recognition |
| Die Anfrage, Die Anfragen | Request |
| Die Angabe, Die Angaben | Indication |
| Die Angabe, Die Angaben | Information, Specification, Indication |
| Die Angelegenheit, Die Angelegenheiten | Affair, Issue |
| Die Angst, Die Ängste | Fear |
| Die Anklage, Die Anklagen | Accusation |
| Die Anklage, Die Anklagen | Prosecution |
| Die Ankündigung, Die Ankündigungen | Announcement |
| Die Anlage, Die Anlagen | Facility (park and castle together) |

| German | English |
| --- | --- |
| Die Anmeldpflicht, Die Anmeldpflichten | Registration Requirement |
| Die Anmeldung, Die Anmeldungen | Registration (for a car, etc.) |
| Die Ansteckung, Die Ansteckungen | Infection, Contagion |
| Die Anstrengung, Die Anstrengungen | Effort |
| Die Antiquität, Die Antiquitäten | Antique |
| Die Antwort, Die Antworten | Answer |
| Die Anwerbung, Die Anwerbungen | Recruitment |
| Die Anwesenheit | Presence |
| Die Anzeige, Die Anzeigen | Advertisement |
| Die Apfelsine, Die Apfelsinen | Orange (fruit) |
| Die Apotheke, Die Apotheken | Pharmacy |
| Die Arbeit, Die Werke | Work |
| Die Arbeitslosigkeit | Unemployment |
| Die Arbeitsplatte, Die Arbeitsplatten | Countertop |
| Die Armee, Die Armeen | Army |
| Die Arroganz | Arrogance |
| Die Art, Die Arten | Type |
| Die Astronomie | Astronomy |
| Die Atombombe, Die Atombomben | Atomic Bomb |
| Die Atomkraft | Nuclear Power (military) |
| Die Aubergine, Die Auberginen | Eggplant |
| Die Auffassung, Die Auffassenungen | View, Opinion |
| Die Aufführung, Die Aufführungen | Performance (art, play, opera) |
| Die Aufgabe, Die Aufgaben | Task |
| Die Auflösung, Die Auflösungen | Resolution (resolved to disband) |
| Die Aufmerksamkeit, Die Aufmerksamkeiten | Attention (focus) |
| Die Aufnahme, Die Aufnahmen | Recording |
| Die Augenbraue, Die Augenbrauen | Eyebrow |
| Die Ausbildung, Die Ausbildungen | Education, Training |
| Die Auseinandersetzung, Die Auseinandersetzungen | Argument, Quarrel |
| Die Auskunft, Die Auskünfte | Information |
| Die Auslosung, Die Auslosungen | Tie, Draw (sports) |
| Die Ausnahme, Die Ausnahmen | Exemption |
| Die Ausrüstung, Die Ausrüstungen | Equipment |
| Die Außenseite, Die Außenseiten | Exterior, Outside |
| Die Aussicht, Die Ansichten | View |
| Die Auster, Die Austern | Oyster |
| Die Auswahl, Die Auswahlen | Choice |
| Die Auswirkung, Die Auswirkungen | Effect (ramification) |
| Die Auswirkung, Die Auswirkungen | Impact |
| Die Auszahlung, Die Auszahlungen | Disbursement, Payout |
| Die Badehosen | Swimming Trunks |
| Die Badewanne, Die Badewannen | Bathtub |

| German | English |
|---|---|
| Die Bakterien | Bacteria |
| Die Banane, Die Bananen | Banana |
| Die Band, Die Bands | Band |
| Die Bank, Die Banken | Bank |
| Die Bar, Die Bars | Bar |
| Die Baustelle, Die Baustellen | Job Site |
| Die Bedeutung, Die Bedeutungen | Meaning |
| Die Bedingung, Die Bedingungen | Condition (of a contract) |
| Die Beerdigung, Die Beerdigung | Funeral |
| Die Beförderung, Die Beförderungen | Promotion (rank) |
| Die Befreiung, Die Befreiungen | Release (hostages) |
| Die Begeisterung, Die Begeisterungen | Enthusiasm |
| Die Behandlung, Die Behandlungen | Treatment |
| Die Beleidigung, Die Beleidigungen | Insult, Affront |
| Die Belohnung, Die Belohnungen | Reward |
| Die Berufsbezeichnung, Die Berufsbezeichnungen | Title (job) |
| Die Besatzung, Die Besatzungen | Crew |
| Die Beschaffung, Die Beschaffungen | Acquisition, Procurement |
| Die Beschäftigung, Die Beschäftigungen | Employment |
| Die Beschießung, Die Beschießungen | Bombardment |
| Die Beschimpfung, Die Beschimpfungen | Abuse |
| Die Beschwerde, Die Beschwerden | Complaint |
| Die Besichtigung, Die Besichtigungen | Viewing, Visual Inspection |
| Die Bestätigung, Die Bestätigungen | Confirmation, Enter at an ATM |
| Die Bestellung, Die Bestellungen | Order (buying or reserving) |
| Die Betonung, Die Betonungen | Emphasis |
| Die Betrachtung, Die Betrachtungen | Reflection, Contemplation |
| Die Bevölkerung, Die Bevölkerungen | Population |
| Die Bewegung, Die Bewegungen | Movement |
| Die Bewerbung, Die Bewerbungen | Job Application |
| Die Bewusstsein, Die Bewusstseine | Awareness |
| Die Bezeichnung, Die Bezeichnungen | Description |
| Die Beziehung, Die Beziehungen | Relationship |
| Die Bibel, Die Bibeln | Bible |
| Die Bibliothek, Die Bibliotheken | Library |
| Die Biene, Die Bienen | Bee |
| Die Biologie | Biology |
| Die Birne, Die Birnen | Pear |
| Die Blase, Die Blasen | Bubble |
| Die Blaskapelle, Die Blasskapellen | Band, Brass |
| Die Blume, Die Blumen | Flower |
| Die Bluse, Die Blusen | Blouse |
| Die Blutwurst, Die Blutwürste | Blood Sausage |

| German | English |
|---|---|
| Die Bob, Die Bobs | Bob (hairstyle) |
| Die Bohne, Die Bohnen | Bean |
| Die Bombardierung, Die Bombardierungen | Bombing |
| Die Börse, Die Börsen | Stock Exchange |
| Die Botschaft, Die Botschaften | Embassy |
| Die Bratsche, Die Bratschen | Viola |
| Die Bratwurst, Die Bratwürste | Bratwurst |
| Die Braut, Die Bräute | Bride |
| Die Bremse, Die Bremsen | Brake |
| Die Brezel, Die Brezeln | Pretzel |
| Die Brille, Die Brillen | Eyeglasses |
| Die Bronzemedaille, Die Bronzemedaillen | Bronze Medal |
| Die Brücke, Die Brücken | Bridge |
| Die Brust, Die Brüste | Breast |
| Die Brust, Die Truhen | Chest (biology) |
| Die Buchhandlung, Die Buchhandlungen | Bookstore |
| Die Bucht, Die Buchten | Bay |
| Die Bühne, Die Bühnen | Stage |
| Die Burg, Die Burgen | Castle, Stronghold, Fortress |
| Die Butter | Butter |
| Die Camoflauge, Die Camoflaugen | Camouflage (clothing) |
| Die Chance, Die Chancen | Chance |
| Die Chancengleichheit, Die Chancengleichheiten | Equal Opportunity |
| Die Chemie | Chemistry |
| Die Christentum | Christianity |
| Die Dame, Die Damen | Lady |
| Die Dame, Die Damen | Madam |
| Die Darstellung, Die Darstellungen | Representation |
| Die Datenbank, Die Datenbanken | Database |
| Die Decke, Die Decken | Blanket |
| Die Decke, Die Decken | Ceiling |
| Die Definition, Die Definitionen | Definition |
| Die Demokratie, Die Demokratien | Democracy |
| Die Demokratische Republik Kongo | Democratic Republic of the Congo (DRC) |
| Die Depression, Die Depressionen | Depression (economics, medical) |
| Die Distanz, Die Distanzen | Distance |
| Die Dividende, Die Dividenden | Dividend (finance) |
| Die Drogerei, Die Drogereien | Drug Store (not pharmacy) |
| Die Drohung, Die Drohungen | Threat |
| Die Dummheit | Foolishness |
| Die Dunkelheit, Die Dunkelheiten | Darkness |
| Die Dusche, Die Duschen | Shower |

| German | English |
|---|---|
| Die Ecke, Die Ecken | Corner |
| Die Effizienz, Die Effizienzen | Efficiency |
| Die Ehe, Die Ehen | Marriage |
| Die Ehefrau, Die Ehefrauen | Wife |
| Die Eifersucht, Die Eifersüchte | Jealousy |
| Die Einbahnstraße, Die Einbahnstraßen | One-way Street |
| Die Einfahrt, Die Einfahrten | Driveway |
| Die Eingliederung, Die Eingliederungen | Integration, Inclusion |
| Die Einheimischen | Locals |
| Die Einheit, Die Einheiten | Unit (military) |
| Die Einigkeit | Unity |
| Die Einkaufstasche, Die Einkaufstaschen | Shopping Bag |
| Die Einlage, Die Einlagen | Deposit (add to or insert) |
| Die Einnahme, Die Einnahmen | Revenue |
| Die Einrichtung, Die Einrichtungen | Facility (furnishings) |
| Die Einstellung, Die Einstellungen | Attitude |
| Die Einstellung, Die Einstellungen | Setting |
| Die Einweihung, Die Einweihungen | Inauguration (of something new) |
| Die Einzahlung, Die Einzahlungen | Deposit (money) |
| Die Elfenbeinküste | Ivory Coast |
| Die Elternschaft | Parenthood |
| Die E-Mail, Die E-Mails | Email |
| Die Ente, Die Enten | Duck |
| Die Entfernung, Die Entfernungen | Distance |
| Die Enthaltsamkeit | Abstinence |
| Die Entscheidung, Die Entscheidungen | Decision |
| Die Entschlusskraft, Die Entschlusskräfte | Resolution (determination) |
| Die Entwicklung, Die Entwicklungen | Development |
| Die Erbse, Die Erbsen | Pea |
| Die Erdbeere, Die Erdbeeren | Strawberry |
| Die Erde, Die Erden | Earth |
| Die Erfahrung, Die Erfahrungen | Experience |
| Die Erhebung, Die Erhebungen | Elevation |
| Die Erinnerung, Die Erinnerungen | Memory |
| Die Erinnerung, Die Erinnerungen | Reminder |
| Die Erkältung, Die Erkältungen | Cold |
| Die Erklärung, Die Erklärungen | Explanation, Declaration |
| Die Eroberung, Die Eroberungen | Conquest |
| Die Errungenschaft, Die Errungenschäfte | Achievement, Attainment |
| Die Erwartung, Die Erwartungen | Expectation |
| Die Erzählung, Die Erzählungen | Story (spoken story, narration) |
| Die Eucharistie | Eucharist |
| Die Ewigkeit, Die Ewigkeiten | Eternity |

| German | English |
|---|---|
| Die Existenz, Die Existenzen | Existence |
| Die Fähigkeit, Die Fähigkeiten | Ability, Skill |
| Die Fahrkarte, Die Fahrkarten | Ticket (for train or bus) |
| Die Familie, Die Familien | Family |
| Die Farbe, Die Farben | Color |
| Die Farbe, Die Farben | Paint |
| Die Fähre, Die Fähren (can add a *Schiff* or *Boot* suffix) | Ferry |
| Die Fastenzeit, Die Fastenzeiten | Fast (fasting time) |
| Die Faust, Die Fäuste | Fist |
| Die Feder, Die Federn | Feather |
| Die Feier, Die Feieren | Celebration, Party |
| Die Feldflasche, Die Feldflaschen | Canteen (camping) |
| Die Festplatte, Die Festplatten | Disk, Hard Drive |
| Die Festung, Die Festungen | Fortress, Fortification |
| Die Feuerwehrfrau, Die Feuerfehrfrauen | Firewoman |
| Die Figur, Die Figuren | Figure (in a play, physical traits) |
| Die Filmkamera, Die Filmkameras | Film Camera |
| Die Fische | Pisces |
| Die Flasche, Die Flaschen | Bottle |
| Die Fledermaus, Die Fledermäuse | Bat |
| Die Flitterwochen (plural used as singular) | Honeymoon |
| Die Flöte, Die Flöten | Flute |
| Die Flotte, Die Flotten | Fleet |
| Die Flugkarte, Die Flugkarten | Plane Ticket |
| Die Flugnummer, Die Flugnummern | Flight Number |
| Die Folge, Die Folgen | Aftermath |
| Die Folge, Die Folgen | Consequence |
| Die Forderung, Die Forderungen | Demand (claim) |
| Die Forelle, Die Forellen | Trout |
| Die Form, Die Formen | Shape |
| Die Form, Die Formen | Form |
| Die Forschung, Die Forschungen | Research |
| Die Frage, Die Fragen | Question |
| Die Frau, Die Frauen | Wife |
| Die Frau, Die Frauen | Woman |
| Die Freiheit | Freedom |
| Die Fremdsprache, Die Fremdsprachen | Foreign Language |
| Die Freude, Die Freuden | Pleasure |
| Die Freundin, Die Freundinnen | Girlfriend |
| Die Freundschaft, Die Freundschaften | Friendship |
| Die Fritteuse, Die Fritteusen | Fryer |
| Die Front, Die Fronten | Front |
| Die Frucht, Die Früchte | Fruit |

| German | English |
|---|---|
| Die Führung, Die Führungen | Guidance |
| Die Führung, Die Führungen | Leadership |
| Die Fülle | Abundance |
| Die Funkstelle, Die Funkstellen | Radio Station |
| Die Funktion, Die Funktionen | Function |
| Die Fußgängerzone, Die Fußgängerzonen | Pedestrian Zone |
| Die Gabel, Die Gabeln | Fork |
| Die Gans, Die Gänse | Goose |
| Die Garagen, Die Garagen | Garage |
| Die Gardine, Die Gardinen | Curtain (thin, allows light through) |
| Die Garnele, Die Garnelen | Shrimp |
| Die Gebühr, Die Gebühren | Fee |
| Die Geduld | Patience |
| Die Gegend, Die Gegenden | Area (living) |
| Die Gegenmaßnahmen, Die Gegenmaßnahmen | Corrective Action, Counter Measures |
| Die Gegenwart | Present (time) |
| Die Geheimzahl, Die Geheimzahlen | PIN (secret number) |
| Die Geige, Die Geigen | Violin |
| Die Gelegenheit, Die Gelegenheiten | Opportunity |
| Die Gemeinde, Die Gemeinden | Municipality |
| Die Gemeinschaft, Die Gemeinschaften | Community |
| Die Genauigkeit, Die Genauigkeiten | Accuracy |
| Die Gepäckausgabe, Die Gepäckausgaben | Baggage Claim |
| Die Gerechtigkeit | Fairness, Righteousness |
| Die Geschichte, Die Geschichten | History |
| Die Geschichte, Die Geschichten | Story (tale) |
| Die Geschwindigkeit, Die Geschwindigkeiten | Speed |
| Die Geschwindigkeitsbegrenzung, Die Geschwindigkeitsbegrenzungen | Speed Limit |
| Die Gesellschaft, Die Gesellschaften | Society |
| Die Gestalt, Die Gestalte | Shape, Form |
| Die Gestaltung, Die Gestaltungen | Arrangement, Design |
| Die Gesundheit | Health |
| Die Gewalt, Die Gewalten | Violence |
| Die Gießpfanne, Die Gießpfannen | Ladle (metallurgy) |
| Die Giraffe, Die Giraffen | Giraffe |
| Die Gitarre, Die Gitarren | Guitar |
| Die Glasur, Die Glasuren | Icing, Glazing |
| Die Gleichberechtigung, Die Gleichberechtigungen | Equal Right |
| Die Glocke, Die Glocken | Bell |
| Die Gnade, Die Gnaden | Grace |
| Die Goldmedaille, Die Goldmedaillen | Gold Medal |

| German | English |
|---|---|
| Die Granate, Die Granaten | Grenade |
| Die Größe, Die Größen | Size, Magnitude |
| Die Großmutter, Die Großmütter | Grandmother |
| Die Großzügigkeit, Die Großzügigkeiten | Generosity |
| Die Gründung, Die Gründungen | Foundation |
| Die Gruppe, Die Gruppen | Group |
| Die Gurke, Die Gurken | Cucumber |
| Die Halbinsel, Die Halbinseln | Peninsula |
| Die Halbzeit, Die Halbzeite | Halftime |
| Die Hälfte, Die Hälften | Half |
| Die Halle, Die Hallen | Hall |
| Die Halskette, Die Halsketten | Necklace |
| Die Haltestelle, Die Haltestellen | Bus stop |
| Die Hand, Die Hände | Hand |
| Die Handfläche, Die Handflächen | Palm |
| Die Handtasche, Die Handtaschen | Handbag |
| Die Haselnuss, Die Haselnüsse | Hazelnut |
| Die Hassrede | Hate Speech |
| Die Hauptrichtung, Die Hauptrichtungen | Mainstream |
| Die Hauptstadt, Die Hauptstädte | Capital |
| Die Hausarbeit, Die Hausarbeiten | Chores, Housework |
| Die Hausaufgaben | Homework |
| Die Haut, Die Häute | Skin |
| Die Hefe, Die Hefen | Yeast |
| Die Heidelbeer, Die Heidelbeeren | Blueberry |
| Die Heimat, Die Heime | Home |
| Die Herausforderung, Die Herausforderungen | Challenge |
| Die Herde, Die Herden | Herd |
| Die Herstellung, Die Herstellungen | Production |
| Die Hilfe, Die Helfin | Help |
| Die Himbeer, Die Himbeeren | Raspberry |
| Die Himmelskunde | Astronomy |
| Die Hitze | Heat |
| Die Hochzeit, Die Hochzeiten | Wedding |
| Die Hochzeitparty, Die Hochzeitpartys | Wedding Reception |
| Die Hoffnung, Die Hoffnungen | Hope |
| Die Höhe, Die Höhen | Height |
| Die Höhenlage, Die Höhenlagen | Altitude |
| Die Höhenzunahme, Die Höhenzunahmen | Height Increase |
| Die Hölle, Die Höllen | Hell |
| Die Hornisse, Die Hornissen | Hornet |
| Die Hose, Die Hosen | Pant |
| Die Idee, Die Ideen | Idea |

| German | English |
|---|---|
| Die Ideologie, Die Ideologien | Ideology |
| Die Industrie, Die Industrien | Industry |
| Die Infektion, Die Infektionen | Infection |
| Die Ingwerwurzel, Die Ingwerwurzeln | Ginger |
| Die Insel, Die Inseln | Island |
| Die Interesse, Die Interessen | Interest |
| Die Investition, Die Investitionen | Investment |
| Die Jacht, Die Jachten | Yacht |
| Die Jacke, Die Jacken | Jacket |
| Die Jahreszeit, Die Jahreszeiten | Season (of the year) |
| Die Jakobsmuschel, Die Jakobsmuscheln | Scallop |
| Die Jeans | Jeans |
| Die Jugendherberge, Die Jugendherbergen | Hostel |
| Die Jungfrau, Die Jungfrauen | Virgo |
| Die Kakerlake, Die Kakerlaken | Cockroach |
| Die Kamera, Die Kameras | Camera |
| Die Kante, Die Kanten | Edge |
| Die Kantine, Die Kantinen | Canteen (snack bar) |
| Die Karotte, Die Karotten | Carrot |
| Die Karte, Die Karten | Card |
| Die Kartoffel, Die Kartoffeln | Potato |
| Die Kaserne, Die Kasernen | Barracks |
| Die Kasse, Die Kassen | Cash Register |
| Die Kassette, Die Kassetten | Cassette |
| Die Kastanie, Die Kastanien | Chestnut |
| Die Katastrophe, Die Katasrophen | Catastrophe |
| Die Katze, Die Katzen | Cat |
| Die Kernkraft, Die Kernkräfte | Nuclear Power (electricity) |
| Die Kerze, Die Kerzen | Candle |
| Die Kette, Die Ketten | Chain |
| Die Kinesiology | Kinesiology |
| Die Kirche, Die Kirchen | Church |
| Die Kirsche, Die Kirschen | Cherry |
| Die Kiste, Die Kisten | Case (large box) |
| Die Kiwi, Die Kiwis | Kiwi |
| Die Klage, Die Klagen | Lawsuit |
| Die Klarinette, Die Klarinetten | Clarinet |
| Die Klasse, Die Klassen | Class |
| Die Klimaanlage, Die Klimaanlagen | Air Conditioner |
| Die Klinge, Die Klingen | Blade |
| Die Kluft, Die Klüfte | Gap, Chasm, Cleft (between things, such as rich and poor) |
| Die Knoblauchpresse, Die Knoblauchpressen | Garlic Press |

| German | English |
|---|---|
| Die Komödie, Die Komödien | Comedy |
| Die Kompetenz, Die Kompetenzen | Competence |
| Die Konfitüre, Die Konfitüren | Jam, Preserves, Fruit Spread |
| Die Königin, Die Königinnen | Queen |
| Die Konserve, Die Konserven | Canned Goods |
| Die Kontrolle, Die Steuerelemente | Control |
| Die Korrektur, Die Korrekturen | Correction |
| Die Kosten, Die Kosten | Cost |
| Die Kostprobe, Die Kostproben | Sample (food) |
| Die Krabbe, Die Krabben | Crab |
| Die Krabbenschere, Die Krabbenscheren | Crab Claw |
| Die Kraft, Die Kräfte | Forces |
| Die Kraft, Die Kräfte | Power, Force |
| Die Krankenschwester, Die Krankenschwestern | Nurse (female) |
| Die Krawatte, Die Krawatten | Necktie |
| Die Kreditvergabe, Die Kreditvergaben | Lending, Loan Activity |
| Die Kreide | Chalk |
| Die Kreuzung, Die Kreuzungen | Intersection |
| Die Kriegskunst | Strategy (military) |
| Die Krücke, Die Krücken | Crutch |
| Die Krustentiere, Die Krustentiere | Crustacean |
| Die Kryptowährung, Die Kryptowährungen | Crypto Currency |
| Die Küche, Die Küchen | Kitchen |
| Die Küchenwaage, Die Küchenwaagen | Kitchen Scale |
| Die Kugel, Die Kugeln | Bullet |
| Die Kuh, Die Kühe | Cow |
| Die Kultur, Die Kulturen | Culture |
| Die Kunst, Die Künste | Art |
| Die Kürbis, Die Kürbisse | Pumpkin |
| Die Küste, Die Küsten | Coast |
| Die Kuvertüre, Die Kuvertüren | Chocolate Coating |
| Die Lage, Die Lagen | Location, Position |
| Die Lage, Die Lagen | Position, Location |
| Die Lage, Die Lagen | Situation |
| Die Lagerung, Die Lagerungen | Storage |
| Die Lampe, Die Lampen | Lamp |
| Die Landebahn, Die Landebahnen | Runway (airport) |
| Die Länge, Die Längen | Length (math, determined by a ruler) |
| Die Last, Die Lasten | Load, Burden |
| Die Laterne, Die Laternen | Lamppost, Streetlight |
| Die Lautstärke, Die Lautstärken | Volume (audio) |
| Die Lava, Die Laven | Lava |

| German | English |
|---|---|
| Die Lebenden | Living |
| Die Lebensmittel | Groceries |
| Die Leidenschaft, Die Leidenschaften | Passion, not passionate |
| Die Leistung, Die Leistungen | Accomplishment |
| Die Leiter, Die Leitern | Ladder |
| Die Leitung, Die Leitungen | Line (telephone) |
| Die Lesung, Die Lesungen | Reading |
| Die Liebe, Die Liebe | Love |
| Die Limone, Die Limonen | Lime |
| Die Linie, Die Linien | Line |
| Die Lippe, Die Lippen | Lip |
| Die List, Die Listen | Deceit, Ruse |
| Die Liste, Die Listen | List |
| Die Literatur, Die Literaturen | Literature |
| Die Lobby, Die Lobbys | Lobby (hotel) |
| Die Lockerung, Die Lockerungen | Easing, Relaxation of |
| Die Lösungen, Die Lösungen | Solution |
| Die Lücke, Die Lücken | Gap, Void (missing piece, such as in knowledge) |
| Die Luft, Die Lüfte | Air |
| Die Luftwaffe, Die Luftwaffen | Air Force |
| Die Lust, Die Lüste | Desire |
| Die Macht, Die Mächte | Might, Power |
| Die Mama, Die Mamas | Mom |
| Die Mandel, Die Mandeln | Almond |
| Die Mango, Die Mangos | Mango |
| Die Manschaft, Die Mannschaften (also Das Team) | Team |
| Die Marine, Die Marinen | Navy |
| Die Marmelade, Die Marmeladen | Marmalade |
| Die Maschine, Die Maschinen | Machine |
| Die Masern | Measles |
| Die Maßeinheit, Die Maßeinheiten | Unit (of measure) |
| Die Maßnahme, Die Maßnahmen | Measure (of action) |
| Die Mathematik | Math, Mathematics |
| Die Mauer, Die Mauern | Wall (as in the Berlin Wall, etc.) |
| Die Medaille, Die Medaillen | Medal |
| Die Medien | Media |
| Die Meeresfrüchte | Seafood (on menus) |
| Die Mehrheit, Die Mehrheiten | Majority |
| Die Meinung, Die Meinungen | Opinion |
| Die Meisterschaft, Die Meisterschaften | Championship |
| Die Meldung, Die Meldungen | Message, Report |
| Die Menge, Die Mengen | Amount, Quantity |

| German | English |
|---|---|
| Die Menge, Die Mengen | Quantity, Amount |
| Die Menschenmasse, Die Menschenmassen | Crowd |
| Die Menschlichkeit, Die Menschlichkeiten | Humanity |
| Die Messe, Die Heilige Messe | Mass, Holy Mass |
| Die Metapher, Die Metaphern | Metaphor |
| Die Methode, Die Methoden | Method |
| Die Miessmuschel, Die Miessmuscheln | Mussel |
| Die Miete, Die Mieten | Rent |
| Die Milch | Milk |
| Die Milliarden | Billions |
| Die Millionen | Millions |
| Die Minderheit, Die Minderheiten | Minority |
| Die Mitgliedschaft, Die Mitgliedschaften | Membership |
| Die Mittagspause, Die Mittagspausen | Lunch Break |
| Die Mittagstunde, Die Mittagstunden | Noon Hour |
| Die Mitte, Die Middles | Middle |
| Die Mitteilung, Die Mitteilungen | Communication, Notice |
| Die Mitternacht | Midnight |
| Die Möbel | Furniture |
| Die Möglichkeit, Die Möglichkeiten | Possibility |
| Die Mongolei | Mongolia |
| Die Motorhaube, Die Motorhauben | Car Hood |
| Die Möwe, Die Möwen | Seagull |
| Die Mücke, Die Mücken | Gnat |
| Die Müdigkeit | Fatigue |
| Die Munition, Die Munitionen | Ammunition |
| Die Münze, Die Münzen | Coins |
| Die Muschel, Die Muscheln | Clam |
| Die Musik, Die Musiken | Music |
| Die Mutter, Die Mütter | Mother |
| Die Nachbarschaft, Die Nachbarschaften | Neighborhood |
| Die Nachfrage, Die Nachfragen | Demand (follow-up question) |
| Die Nachlässigkeit, Die Nachlässigkeiten | Negligence |
| Die Nachricht, Die Nachrichten | Message |
| Die Nachrichten | News |
| Die Nacht, Die Nächte | Night |
| Die Nachtschicht, Die Nachtschicht | Night Shift |
| Die Nadel, Die Nadeln | Needle |
| Die Nase, Die Nasen | Nose |
| Die Natur, Die Naturen | Nature |
| Die Neurose, Die Neurosen | Neurotic |
| Die Nichte, Die Nichten | Niece |
| Die Niederlande | Netherlands |

| German | English |
| --- | --- |
| Die Niederlassung, Die Niederlassungen | Branch (of an organization) |
| Die Notbremse, Die Notbremsen | Emergency Brake |
| Die Note, Die Noten | Note (school grade, banknote, musical) |
| Die Notiz, Die Notizen | Note |
| Die Nudel, Die Nudeln | Noodle |
| Die Nummer, Die Nummern | Number |
| Die Nuss, Die Nüsse | Nut |
| Die Oberfläche, Die Oberflächen | Surface |
| Die Oboe, Die Oboen | Oboe |
| Die Öffentlichkeit | Public |
| Die Oligarchie, Die Oligarchien | Oligarchy |
| Die Olympiade, Die Olympiaden | Olympic Games |
| Die Operation, Die Operationen | Operation (medical) |
| Die Ordentlichkeit | Orderliness |
| Die Ordnung | Order, Tidiness |
| Die Orgel, Die Orgeln | Organ, Music |
| Die Panne, Die Pannen | Tire (flat) |
| Die Paprika | Paprika |
| Die Paprika, Die Paprikas | Pepper (bell) |
| Die Parfümerie, Die Parfümerien | Cosmetic Store |
| Die Partei, Die Parteien | Party (political) |
| Die Party, Die Partys | Party (fun) |
| Die Pause, Die Pausen | Pause or Break |
| Die Person, Die Personen | Person |
| Die Personalkürzung, Die Personalkürzung | Layoff |
| Die Persönlichkeit, Die Persönlichkeiten | Personality |
| Die Pfeife, Die Pfeifen | Fife, Whistle |
| Die Pflaume, Die Pflaumen | Plum (round, sweet) |
| Die Pflege | Care |
| Die Pflicht, Die Pflichten | Obligation, Duty |
| Die Pfote, Die Pfoten | Paw |
| Die Philosophie, Die Philosophien | Philosophy |
| Die Piccoloflöte, Die Piccoloflöten | Piccolo |
| Die Pistole, Die Pistolen | Pistol |
| Die Pizza, Die Pizzas | Pizza |
| Die Planung, Die Planungen | Planning |
| Die Polizei, Die Polizeien (plural is rare) | Police |
| Die Posaune, Die Posaunen | Trombone |
| Die Post | Mail |
| Die Praxis, Die Praktiken | Practice (as in medical practice) |
| Die Preisgestaltung, Die Preisgestaltungen | Pricing |
| Die Presse, Die Pressen | Squeezer |
| Die Priorität, Die Prioritäten | Priority |

| German | English |
|---|---|
| Die Prognose, Die Prognosen | Prognosis |
| Die Prüfung, Die Prüfungen | Test (school, verification) |
| Die Psychologie | Psychology |
| Die Qualität, Die Qualitäten | Quality |
| Die Qualle, Die Quallen | Jellyfish |
| Die Quelle, Die Quellen | Source |
| Die Quittung, Die Quittungen | Receipt |
| Die Radierung, Die Radierungen | Etching |
| Die Radmutter, Die Radmuttern | Lug Nuts |
| Die Rast, Die Reste | Rest |
| Die Ratte, Die Ratten | Rat |
| Die Raum, Die Räume | Room (space) |
| Die Reaktion, Die Reaktionen | Reaction, Response |
| Die Rechnung, Die Rechnungen | Bill |
| Die Rechnung, Die Rechnungen | Check |
| Die Rede, Die Reden | Speech, Address |
| Die Regeln | Policies (also see Regulation) |
| Die Regierung, Die Regierungen | Government |
| Die Reibung, Die Reibungen | Friction |
| Die Reihe, Die Reihen | Row |
| Die Reise, Die Reisen | Trip |
| Die Religion, Die Religionen | Religion |
| Die Republik, Die Republiken | Republic |
| Die Rettung, Die Rettungen | Rescue |
| Die Revolution, Die Revolutionen | Revolution (uprising) |
| Die Rezession, Die Rezessionen | Recession |
| Die Richtlinie, Die Richtlinien | Guideline |
| Die Richtung, Die Richtungen | Direction |
| Die Rocky Mountains | Rocky Mountains |
| Die Rolle, Die Rollen | Role (theater, not function) |
| Die Romantik | Romanticism |
| Die Rose, Die Rosen | Rose |
| Die Rosine, Die Rosinen | Raisin |
| Die Rückkehr | Return |
| Die Rückkoppelung, Die Rückkoppelungen | Feedback (sound, guitar) |
| Die Rückmeldung, Die Rückmeldungen | Feedback |
| Die Runden, Die Runden | Laps, sport |
| Die Rundfahrt, Die Rundfahrten | Roundtrip |
| Die Saison, Die Saisons | Season (for sport, theater, etc.) |
| Die Saite, Die Saiten | String (instrument) |
| Die Schachtel, Die Schachteln | Box |
| Die Schafe | Sheep |
| Die Schaffung, Die Schaffungen | Creation (establishment of, as in jobs) |

| German | English |
| --- | --- |
| Die Schale, Die Schalen | Bowl |
| Die Scheidung, Die Scheidungen | Divorce |
| Die Scheiße, Die Scheiße | Shit |
| Die Schere, Die Scheren | Scissor |
| Die Schichtarbeit, Die Schichtarbeiten | Shift Work |
| Die Schildkröte, Die Schildkröten | Turtle |
| Die Schlacht, Die Schlachten | Battle |
| Die Schlange, Die Schlangen | Snake |
| Die Schminke (example: *Ich schminke mich*) | Makeup Items |
| Die Schnelle, Die Schnellen | Velocity |
| Die Schnur, Die Schnüre | String, Cord |
| Die Schokolade, Die Schokoladen | Chocolate |
| Die Schönheit, Die Schönheiten | Beauty |
| Die Schöpfkelle, Die Schöpfkellen | Ladle (food) |
| Die Schöpfung, Die Schöpfungen | Creation (as in of the world, ex nihilo) |
| Die Schrift, Die Schriften | Scripture |
| Die Schrift, Die Schriften | Writing |
| Die Schublade, Die Schubladen | Drawer |
| Die Schuhcreme, Die Schuhcremes | Shoe Polish |
| Die Schuld, Die Schulden | Debt |
| Die Schuldenbremse, Die Schuldenbremsen | Debt Limit |
| Die Schulter, Die Schultern | Shoulder |
| Die Schwäche, Die Schwächen | Weakness |
| Die Schwangerschaft, Die Schwangerschaften | Pregnancy |
| Die Schwarzarbeit, Die Schwarzarbeiten | Moonlighting |
| Die Schweiz | Switzerland |
| Die Schwester, Die Schwestern | Sister |
| Die Schwiegermutter, Die Schwiegermütter | Mother-in-law |
| Die Schwierigkeit, Die Schwierigkeiten | Difficulty |
| Die See, Die Seen | Sea |
| Die Seele, Die Seelen | Soul |
| Die Sehenswürdigkeit, Die Sehenswürdigkeiten | Sight (as in "see the sights") |
| Die Seite, Die Seiten | Page |
| Die Seite, Die Seiten | Side |
| Die Seitenlinie, Die Seitenlinien | Sideline (sport) |
| Die Sekunde, Die Sekunden | Second (time) |
| Die Selbständigkeit | Independence, Self-Reliance |
| Die Show, Die Shows | Show |
| Die Sicherheit | Safety |
| Die Siedlung, Die Siedlungen | Settlement |
| Die Silbermedaille, Die Silbermedaillen | Silver Medal |
| Die Silbermünze, Die Silbermünzen | Silver Coin |

| German | English |
| --- | --- |
| Die Sitzung, Die Sitzungen | Meeting (sitting down) |
| Die Slowakei | Slovakia |
| Die SMS-Nachricht (or just Die SMS), Die SMS-Nachrichten | Text Message |
| Die Socke, Die Socken | Sock |
| Die Software, Die Softwares | Software |
| Die Soja, Die Sojen | Soy |
| Die Sonderangebot, Die Sonderangebote | Special Offers |
| Die Sonne, Die Sonnen | Sun |
| Die Sorge, Die Sorgen | Worry, Concern |
| Die Sorte, Die Sorten | Variety |
| Die Soße, Die Soßen | Sauce, Gravy |
| Die Speise, Die Speisen | Food |
| Die Speisestärke | Corn Starch (thickener) |
| Die Spinne, Die Spinnen | Spider |
| Die Spitze, Die Spitzen | Top |
| Die Sprache, Die Sprachen | Language |
| Die Spule, Die Spulen | Spool, Reel |
| Die Stabilität, Die Stabilitäten | Stability |
| Die Stachelbeere, Die Stachelbeeren | Gooseberry |
| Die Stadion, Die Stadien | Stadium |
| Die Stadt, Die Städte | City |
| Die Stadt, Die Städte | Town |
| Die Station, Die Stationen | Station (transit) |
| Die Statue, Die Statuen | Statue |
| Die Stechmücke, Die Stechmücken (also Der Moskito) | Mosquito |
| Die Steigerung, Die Steigerungen (from steigen) | Increase (climb) |
| Die Stelle, Die Stellen | Position (at work) |
| Die Stellung, Die Stellungen | Position (stance) |
| Die Sternkunde | Astronomy |
| Die Steuer, Die Steuern | Tax |
| Die Stieftochter, Die Stieftöchter | Stepdaughter |
| Die Stille, Die Stille | Silence |
| Die Stimme, Die Stimmen | Voice, Vote |
| Die Stirn, Die Stirnen | Forehead |
| Die Strafe, Die Strafen | Punishment, Penalty, Sentence |
| Die Strandwache, Die Strandwachen | Beachguard |
| Die Straße, Die Straßen | Road |
| Die Straße, Die Straßen | Street |
| Die Strategie, Die Strategien | Strategy (general, civilian) |
| Die Strecke, Die Strecken | Stretch (of road) |
| Die Strömung, Die Strömungen | Current (water) |
| Die Stunde, Die Stunden | Hour |

| German | English |
|---|---|
| Die Stute, Die Stuten | Mare |
| Die Substanz, Die Substanzen | Matter, Substance |
| Die Suche, Die Suchen | Quest, Search |
| Die Suppe, Die Suppen | Soup |
| Die Süßkartoffel, Die Süßkartoffeln | Sweet Potato |
| Die Szene, Die Szenen | Scene |
| Die Tafel, Die Tafeln | Board (or type of table, flat piece) |
| Die Tagesordnung, Die Tagesordnungen | Agenda |
| Die Tante, Die Tanten | Aunt |
| Die Tarnung, Die Tarnungen | Camouflage (cover, to hide) |
| Die Tasche, Die Taschen | Pocket |
| Die Tasse, Die Tassen | Cup |
| Die Tastatur, Die Tastaturen | Keyboard |
| Die Tat, Die Taten | Deed, Act |
| Die Tätigkeit, Die Tätigkeiten | Deeds |
| Die Tatsache, Die Tatsachen | Fact |
| Die Taufe, Die Taufen | Baptism |
| Die Technologie, Die Technologien | Technology |
| Die Teilzeitarbeit | Part-time Work |
| Die Terrasse, Die Terrassen | Deck |
| Die Theorie, Die Theorien | Theory |
| Die Tiefe, Die Tiefen | Depth |
| Die Titelseite | Magazine Cover |
| Die Tochter, Die Töchter | Daughter |
| Die Tradition, Die Traditionen | Tradition |
| Die Träne, Die Tränen | Tear (crying) |
| Die Traube, Die Trauben | Grape |
| Die Trennung, Die Trennungen | Separation |
| Die Treppe, Die Treppen | Stair |
| Die Trommel, Die Trommeln | Drum |
| Die Trompete, Die Trompeten | Trumpet |
| Die Truppe, Die Truppen | Troop |
| Die Tür, Die Türen | Door |
| Die Türkei | Turkey |
| Die Türklingel, Die Türklingeln | Doorbell |
| Die Turnhall, Die Turnhallen | Gym, School |
| Die Türöffnung, Die Türöffnungen | Doorway |
| Die Türschwelle, Die Türschwellen | Doorstep |
| Die Übergabe, Die Übergaben | Handover |
| Die Überlegenheit, Die Überlegenheiten | Superiority |
| Die Überraschung, Die Überraschungen | Surprise |
| Die Übersetzung, Die Übersetzungen | Translation |
| Die Überstunde, Die Überstunden | Overtime |

| German | English |
|---|---|
| Die Überwindung, Die Überwindungen | Overcoming |
| Die Überzeugung, Die Überzeugungen | Conviction (convinced) |
| Die Übung, Die Übungen | Practice (to improve a skill) |
| Die Uhr, Die Uhren | Clock |
| Die Umdrehung, Die Umdrehungen | Revolution (per minute) |
| Die Umkehr | Reversal, Turning Back (for example, yield curve) |
| Die Umkehrung, Die Umkehrungen | Inversion |
| Die Umsiedlung, Die Umsiedlungen | Resettlement |
| Die Umweltverschmutzung, Die Umweltverschmutzungen | Pollution (environment) |
| Die Unabhängigkeit | Independence, 4th of July |
| Die Unendlichkeit, Die Unendlichkeiten | Infinity |
| Die Unfähigkeit, Die Unfähigkeiten | Inability |
| Die Universität, Die Universitäten | University |
| Die Unordentlichkeit | Mess, Untidiness, Clutter |
| Die Unterbrechung, Die Unterbrechungen | Interruption |
| Die Unterdrückung, Die Unterdrückungen | Suppression, Oppression |
| Die Unterhaltung, Die Unterhaltungen | Conversation (casual) |
| Die Unterkunft, Die Unterkünfte | Accommodation, Housing |
| Die Unterrichtung, Die Unterrichtungen | Instruction, Information |
| Die Unterschrift, Die Unterschriften | Signature |
| Die Unterwäsche, Die Unterkleidung | Underwear |
| Die Ursache, Die Ursachen | Cause |
| Die Verabschiedung, Die Verabschiedungen | Farewell, Sendoff |
| Die Veranda, Die Veranden | Porch, Veranda |
| Die Verantwortung, Die Verantwortungen | Responsibility |
| Die Veräußerung, Die Veräußerungen | Divestment, Sale |
| Die Vereinbarung, Die Vereinbarungen | Agreement |
| Die Vereinigten Arabischen Emirate | United Arab Emirates |
| Die Vereinigten Staaten, Die USA | United States |
| Die Vergabe, Die Vergaben | Allocate Credit |
| Die Vergabe, Die Vergaben | Award (contract), Allocate |
| Die Vergangenheit | Past |
| Die Verhandlung, Die Verhandlungen | Negotiation |
| Die Verlassenheit | Abandonment |
| Die Verleugnung, Die Verleugnungen | Refutation |
| Die Verlobung, Die Verlobung | Engagement |
| Die Vernachlässigung, Die Vernachlässigungen | Neglect |
| Die Vernichtung, Die Vernichtungen | Destruction (annihilation) |
| Die Verordnung, Die Verordnungen | Decree |
| Die Verpflegung, Die Verpflegungen | Subsistence |
| Die Verpflichtung, Die Verpflichtungen | Commitment |
| Die Versammlung, Die Versammlungen | Assembly, Gathering |

| German | English |
|---|---|
| Die Verschmutzung, Die Verschmutzungen | Contamination |
| Die Versicherung, Die Versicherungen | Insurance |
| Die Version, Die Versionen | Version |
| Die Verspätung, Die Verspätungen | Delay |
| Die Verteilung, Die Verteilungen | Distribution |
| Die Verwaltungen, Die Verwaltungen | Administration |
| Die Verwirrung, Die Verwirrungen | Confusion |
| Die Vielfalt | Diversity |
| Die Vision, Die Visionen | Vision |
| Die Volksvertretung, Die Volksvertretungen | Parliament, People's Representation |
| Die Vollzeitarbeit | Full-time Work |
| Die Voraussage, Die Voraussagen | Prediction (prophecy, like Nostradamus) |
| Die Voraussetzung, Die Voraussetzungen | Prerequisites |
| Die Vorbereitung, Die Vorbereitungen | Preparation |
| Die Vorhalle, Die Vorhallen | Porch, Vestibule |
| Die Vorhersage, Die Vorhersagen | Prediction (forecast) |
| Die Vorlage, Die Vorlagen | Template, Model |
| Die Vorlesung, Die Vorlesungen | Lecture, University |
| Die Vorstellungskraft, Die Vorstellungskräfte | Imagination |
| Die Vorzug, Die Vorzüge | Virtue, Benefit, Value, Merit |
| Die Vorzugsbehandlung, Die Vorzugsbehandlungen | Preferential Treatment |
| Die Waage, Die Waagen | Libra |
| Die Waage, Die Waagen | Scale (to weigh) |
| Die Waffe, Die Waffen | Gun |
| Die Waffe, Die Waffen | Weapon |
| Die Wahl, Die Wahlen | Choice (election, also what you choose) |
| Die Wahl, Die Wahlen | Election |
| Die Wahl, Die Wahlen | Vote (between choices) |
| Die Wahrheit, Die Wahrheiten | Truth |
| Die Wahrnehmung, Die Wahrnehmungen | Perception |
| Die Währung, Die Währungen | Currency |
| Die Wand, Die Wände | Wall (inside) |
| Die Wandelhalle, Die Wandelhallen | Foyer |
| Die Wange, Die Wangen | Cheek |
| Die Ware, Die Waren | Product (goods) |
| Die Warnung, Die Warnungen | Warning |
| Die Wartung, Die Wartungen | Maintenance (preventive) |
| Die Wassermelone, Die Wassermelonen | Watermelon |
| Die Website, Die Websites | Website |
| Die Welle, Die Wellen | Wave |

| German | English |
|--------|---------|
| Die Welt, Die Welt | World |
| Die Weltanschauung, Die Weltanschauungen | Worldview, Ideology |
| Die Weltwirtschaft, Die Weltwirtschaften | Global Economy |
| Die Wende, Die Windungen | Turn |
| Die Wespe, Die Wespen | Wasp |
| Die Wettbewerbsfähigkeit, Die Wettbewerbsfähigkeiten | Competitiveness |
| Die Wettervorhersagen, Die Wettervorhersagen | Weather Forecast |
| Die Wichtigkeit | Importance |
| Die Wiederherstellung, Die Wiederherstellungen | Restoration |
| Die Wiese, Die Wiesen | Meadow |
| Die Wimper, Die Wimpern | Eyelash |
| Die Wimperntusche, Die Wimperntuschen | Mascara |
| Die Windschutzscheibe, Die Windschutzscheiben | Windshield |
| Die Wirklichkeit, Die Wirklichkeiten | Reality |
| Die Wirkung, Die Wirkungen | Effect (impact) |
| Die Wirtschaft, Die Wirtschaften | Economy |
| Die Wirtschaftswissenhaften (used with singular verbs) | Economics |
| Die Wissenschaft, Die Wissenschaften | Science |
| Die Witwe, Die Witwen | Widow |
| Die Woche, Die Wochen | Week |
| Die Wohltätigkeit, Die Wohltätigkeiten | Charity (wholesome deeds) |
| Die Wohltätigkeitsorganisation, Die Wohltätigkeitsorganisationen | Charity (organization) |
| Die Wohnung, Die Wohnungen | Apartment |
| Die Wolke, Die Wolken | Cloud |
| Die Würde | Dignity |
| Die Wurst, Die Würste | Sausage |
| Die Wurzel, Die Wurzeln | Root |
| Die Zahl, Die Zählen | Number |
| Die Zahlung, Die Zahlungen | Payment |
| Die Zange, Die Zangen | Tongs |
| Die Zecke, Die Zecken | Tick (insect) |
| Die Zeichen, Die Zeichen | Sign (graphic, drawn) |
| Die Zeichnung, Die Zeichnungen | Drawing |
| Die Zeit, Die Zeiten | Time |
| Die Zeitschrift, Die Zeitschriften | Magazine |
| Die Zeitung, Die Zeitungen | Newspaper |
| Die Zelle, Die Zellen | Cell |
| Die Zersetzung, Die Zersetzungen | Decomposition, Disintegration |

| German | English |
|---|---|
| Die Zerstörung, Die Zerstörungen | Destruction (demolition) |
| Die Ziege, Die Ziegen | Goat |
| Die Ziffer, Die Ziffern | Numeral, Cypher |
| Die Zigarre, Die Zigarren | Cigar |
| Die Zigarrette, Die Zigarretten | Cigarette |
| Die Zitrone, Die Zitronen | Lemon |
| Die Zone, Die Zonen | Zone |
| Die Zucchini, Die Zucchini | Zucchini |
| Die Zufriedenheit | Satisfaction |
| Die Zugehörigkeit, Die Zugehörigkeiten | Affiliation, Party, Club |
| Die Zuhörer (different from Der Zuhörer) | Audience |
| Die Zukunft | Future |
| Die Zunahme, Die Zunahmen (from *zunehmen*) | Increase (add to) |
| Die Zunge, Die Zungen | Tongue |
| Die Zurückhaltung | Restraint |
| Die Zusammenarbeit | Cooperation |
| Die Zustimmung, Die Zustimmungen | Consent, Agreement |
| Die Zutat, Die Zutaten | Ingredient |
| Die Zwetschge, Die Zwetschgen | Plum (oval, tart hybrid) |
| no singular, Die Daten | Data |
| no singular, Die Klamotten | Clothes, Gear |
| no singular, Die Kleider | Clothes |
| no singular, Die Religiösen | Religious (usually an adjective) |
| no singular, Die Süßigkeiten | Sweets (not baked) |
| no singular, Die Wehen | Contractions, Labor Pains |

# NEUTER (*DAS*) NOUNS

| German | English |
|---|---|
| Das Abendessen, Die Abendessen | Dinner |
| Das Abendmahl, Die Kommunion | Communion |
| Das Abenteuer, Die Abenteuer | Adventure |
| Das Abgeordnetenhaus | House of Representatives |
| Das Abitur | Final Exam (academic high school) |
| Das Abkommen, Die Abkommen | Deal, Agreement (political) |
| Das Abkommen, Die Abkommen | Pact |
| Das Abseits, Die Abseits | Offsides (sports) |
| Das Abwasser | Sewage |
| Das Adjektiv, Die Adjektive | Adjective |
| Das All | Universe |
| Das Alphabet, Die Alphabete | Alphabet |
| Das Alte, Die Alte | Age |
| Das Altertum | Antiquity |
| Das Angebot, Die Angebote | Offer |
| Das Anliegen, Die Anliegen | Concern, Issue |
| Das Ansehen | Reputation |
| Das Anwesen, Die Anwesen | Estate, Property |
| Das Arabisch | Arabic (language) |
| Das Aramäisch | Aramaic (language) |
| Das Ärgernis, Die Ärgernisse | Annoyance |
| Das Argument, Die Argumente | Argument (statement to convince) |
| Das Armenisch | Armenian (language) |
| Das Arzneimittel, Die Arzneimittel | Drug (pharmacy) |
| Das Atom, Die Atome | Atom |
| Das Auge, Die Augen | Eye |
| Das Ausmaß, Die Ausmaße | Extent |
| Das Aussehen | Appearance |
| Das Auto, Die Autos | Car |
| Das Autorennen, Die Autorennen | Car Race |
| Das Baby, Die Babys | Baby |
| Das Backblech, Die Backbleche | Baking Sheet |
| Das Bad, Die Badezimmer | Bathroom |
| Das Badetuch, Die Badetücher | Towel (bath) |
| Das Bargeld | Cash |
| Das Bedürfnis, Die Bedürfnisse | Need |
| Das Bein, Die Beine | Leg |
| Das Beispiel, Die Beispiele | Example |
| Das Benzin, Die Benzine | Gas, Petrol |
| Das Betäubungsmittel, Die Betäubungsmittel | Narcotic |

| German | English |
|---|---|
| Das Bett, Die Betten | Bed |
| Das Bewusstsein | Consciousness |
| Das Bier, Die Biere | Beer |
| Das Bild, Die Bilder | Image |
| Das Bild, Die Bilder | Picture |
| Das Blatt, Die Blätter | Leaf |
| Das Blatt, Die Blätter | Sheet |
| Das Blech, Die Bleche | Sheet Metal |
| Das Blei | Lead (metal) |
| Das Blut, Die Blut | Blood |
| Das Bombardment, Die Bombardments | Bombardment |
| Das Bonbon, Die Bonbons | Candy |
| Das Boot, Die Boote | Boat |
| Das Bremslicht, Die Bremslichter | Brake Light |
| Das Brot, Die Brote | Bread |
| Das Buch, Die Bücher | Book |
| Das Buchregale, Die Bücherregale | Bookshelf |
| Das Bulgarisch | Bulgarian (language) |
| Das Büro, Die Büros | Office |
| Das Café, Die Cafés | Café |
| Das Cello, Die Cellos | Cello |
| Das Chinesisch | Chinese (language) |
| Das College, Die Colleges | College |
| Das Computerteil, Die Computerteile | Hardware, Part, Component (computer) |
| Das Couch, Die Couchen | Couch |
| Das Dach, Die Dächer | Roof |
| Das Dänisch | Danish (language) |
| Das Datum, Die Daten | Date |
| Das Detail, Die Details | Detail |
| Das Deutsch | German (language) |
| Das Ding, Die Dinge | Thing |
| Das Doppelzimmer, Die Doppelzimmer | Double Room |
| Das Dorf, Die Dörfer | Village |
| Das Dreieck, Die Dreiecke | Triangle |
| Das Dunkel | Dark |
| Das Ehepaar, Die Ehepaare | Married Couple |
| Das Ehepaar, Die Paare | Couple |
| Das Ei, Die Eier | Egg |
| Das Eichörnchen, Die Eichhörnchen | Squirrel |
| Das Eigelb (example: *drei Eigelb*) | Egg Yolk |
| Das Eigentum, Die Eigentume | Property |
| Das Einkaufszentrum, Die Einkaufszentren | Mall |
| Das Einkommen, Die Einkommen | Income, Earnings |

| German | English |
|---|---|
| Das Einzelzimmer, Die Einzelzimmer | Single Room |
| Das Eis | Ice |
| Das Eiweiß (example: *drei Eiweiß*) | Egg White |
| Das Elektron, Die Elektronen | Electron |
| Das Elend | Hardship, Misery |
| Das Eltern, Die Eltern | Parent |
| Das Elterngeld, Die Elterngelder | Parental Allowance |
| Das Ende, Die Enden | End |
| Das Englisch | English (language) |
| Das Erdbeben, Die Erdbeben | Earthquake |
| Das Ereignis, Die Ereignisse | Event |
| Das Ergebnis, Die Ergebnisse | Outcome, Result |
| Das Ergebnis, Die Ergebnisse | Result |
| Das Erlebnis, Die Erlebnisse | Experience |
| Das Erzeugnis, Die Erzeugnisse | Product (business) |
| Das Essen | Food |
| Das Estnisch | Estonian (language) |
| Das Exam, Die Examen | Exam |
| Das Export | Lager, Beer |
| Das Fach, Die Fäche | Compartment |
| Das Fach, Die Fäche | Subject (a discipline of study or a department) |
| Das Fach, Die Fächer | Pocket (in a bag) |
| Das Fachwerkhaus, Die Fachwerkhäuser | House (timbered) |
| Das Fahrrad, Die Fahrräder | Bicycle |
| Das Fahrzeug, Die Fahrzeuge | Vehicle |
| Das Feedback, Die Feedbacks | Feedback |
| Das Feld, Die Felder | Field |
| Das Fenster, Die Fenster | Window |
| Das Fernseher, Die Fernseher | Television |
| Das Fest, Die Feste | Festival |
| Das Fett, Die Fette | Fat (for cooking) |
| Das Feuer, Die Feuer | Fire |
| Das Fieber, Die Fieber | Fever |
| Das Finnisch | Finnish (language) |
| Das Fitnessstudio, Die Fitnessstudios | Gym (commercial) |
| Das Fleisch | Meat, Flesh |
| Das Flughafenterminal, Die Flughafenterminals | Airport Terminal |
| Das Flugzeug, Die Flugzeuge | Airplane |
| Das Formular, Die Formulare | Form (paper) |
| Das Forum, Die Foren | Forum |
| Das Foto, Die Fotos | Photo |
| Das Französisch | French (language) |

| German | English |
|---|---|
| Das Friesisch | Frisian (language) |
| Das Frucht, Die Früchte | Fruit |
| Das Frühjahr | Spring |
| Das Frühstück, Die Frühstücke | Breakfast |
| Das Fußballtor, Die Fußballtore | Soccer Goal |
| Das Gähnen | Yawn |
| Das Gälisch | Gaelic (language) |
| Das Garn, Die Garne | Yarn |
| Das Gebäck | Pastry, Pastries |
| Das Gebäude, Die Gebäude | Building |
| Das Gebiet, Die Gebiete | Area (larger) |
| Das Gebiet, Die Gebiete | Region |
| Das Gebot, Die Gebote | Commandment |
| Das Gedächtnis, Die Gedächtnisse | Memory, not electronic |
| Das Gedicht, Die Gedichte | Poem |
| Das Gefängnis, Die Gefängnisse | Prison |
| Das Gefäß, Die Gefäße | Vessel (kitchen) |
| Das Gefüge, Die Gefüge | Texture, Arrangement |
| Das Gefühl, Die Gefühle | Emotion |
| Das Gefühl, Die Gefühle | Feeling |
| Das Gegengewicht, Die Gegengewichte | Counterweight |
| Das Gegenteil, Die Gegenteile | Opposite |
| Das Gehalt, Die Gehälter | Salary |
| Das Gehalt, Die Gehälter | Wage, Pay, Earnings |
| Das Geheimnis, Die Geheimnisse | Secret |
| Das Gehirn, Die Gehirne | Brain |
| Das Gehör, Die Gehöre | Hearing |
| Das Geld, Die Gelder | Money |
| Das Gelee, Die Gelees | Jelly |
| Das Gemälde, Die Gemälde | Painting |
| Das Gemüse, Die Gemüse | Vegetable |
| Das Gemüssemesser, Die Gemüssemesser | Paring Knife |
| Das Gen, Die Gene | Gene |
| Das Genus, Die Genera | Gender (language) |
| Das Gepäck | Luggage |
| Das Geräusch, Die Geräusche | Noise |
| Das Geräusch, Die Geräusche | Sound (non-musical) |
| Das Gericht, Die Gerichte | Court |
| Das Geschäft, Die Geschäfte | Shop, Store |
| Das Geschenk, Die Geschenke | Gift |
| Das Geschlecht, Die Geschlechter | Gender (sex) |
| Das Gesetz, Die Gesetze | Law |
| Das Gesicht, Die Gesichter | Face |

| German | English |
| --- | --- |
| Das Gespräch, Die Gespräche | Conversation (not personal) |
| Das Getränk, Die Getränke | Beverage, Drink |
| Das Gewicht, Die Gewichte | Weight |
| Das Gewitter, Die Gewitter | Thunderstorm |
| Das Gewürz, Die Gewürze | Spice, Seasoning |
| Das Glas, Die Gläser | Glass |
| Das Glied, Die Glieder | Limb (anatomy) |
| Das Glockenspiel, Die Glockenspiele | Chimes |
| Das Gold | Gold |
| Das Gras, Die Gräser | Grass |
| Das Griechisch | Greek (language) |
| Das Gros, Die Grosse | Bulk, Gross |
| Das Gutschein, Die Gutscheine | Coupon |
| Das Haar, Die Haare | Hair |
| Das Handeln | Action |
| Das Handtuch, Die Handtücher | Towel (hand) |
| Das Handy, Die Handys | Cellphone |
| Das Haupt, Die Häupter | Main, Head, Primary (as a prefix) |
| Das Hauptfach, Die Hauptfächer | Major (college) |
| Das Haus, Die Häuser | House |
| Das Haushaltswarengeschäft, Die Haushaltswarengeschäfte | Hardware Store |
| Das Hebräisch | Hebrew (language) |
| Das Heim, Die Heime | Home, Asylum |
| Das Hemd, Die Hemden | Shirt |
| Das Herz, Die Herzen | Heart |
| Das Heu | Hay |
| Das Hindernis, Die Hindernisse | Hindrance |
| Das Hindernis, Die Hindernisse | Obstacle |
| Das Hindi | Hindi (language) |
| Das Holz | Wood (woodwork) |
| Das Höschen, Die Höschen | Panties |
| Das Hotel, Die Hotels | Hotel |
| Das Huhn, Die Hühner | Chicken |
| Das Imperium, Die Imperien | Empire |
| Das Innere | Owner |
| Das Insekt, Die Insekten | Insect |
| Das Internet | Internet |
| Das Isländisch | Icelandic (language) |
| Das Italienisch | Italian (language) |
| Das Jahr, Die Jahre | Year |
| Das Jahrbuch, Die Jahrbücher | Yearbook |
| Das Japanisch | Japanese (language) |

| German | English |
|---|---|
| Das Kalkül, Die Kalküle | Calculation |
| Das Känguru, Die Kängurus | Kangaroo |
| Das Kaninchen, Die Kaninchen | Rabbit |
| Das Kanu, Die Kanus | Canoe |
| Das Kap, Die Kaps | Cape |
| Das Kapital | Capital |
| Das Kapitel, Die Kapitel | Chapter |
| Das Kaufhaus, Die Kaufhäuser | Department Store |
| Das Kennzeichenschild, Die Kennzeichenschilder | License Plate |
| Das Kernkraftwerk, Die Kernkraftwerke | Nuclear Power Plant |
| Das Kind, Die Kinder | Child |
| Das Kinderbuch, Die Kinderbüche | Children's Book |
| Das Kinn, Die Kinne | Chin |
| Das Kino, Die Kinos | Cinema |
| Das Kissen, Die Kissen | Pillow |
| Das Klassenzimmer, Die Klassenzimmer | Classroom |
| Das Klavier, Die Klaviere | Piano |
| Das Kleid, Die Kleider | Dress |
| Das Klima, Die Klimas | Climate |
| Das Knie, Die Knie | Knee |
| Das Konto, Die Konten | Account |
| Das Konzert, Die Konzerte | Concert |
| Das Koreanisch | Korean (language) |
| Das Krankenhaus, Die Krankenhäuser | Hospital |
| Das Kreuz, Die Kreuze | Cross |
| Das Kreuzworträtsel, Die Kreuzworträtsel | Crossword Puzzle |
| Das Küken, Die Küken | Chick, Baby Chicken |
| Das Kupfer | Copper |
| Das Kurdisch | Kurdish (language) |
| Das Lächeln, Die Lächeln | Smile |
| Das Lager, Die Lager | Camp |
| Das Lamm, Die Lämmer | Lamb |
| Das Land, Die Länder | Country |
| Das Land, Die Ländereien | Land |
| Das Landgut, Die Landgüter | Manor, Estate |
| Das Latein | Latin (language) |
| Das Leben, Die Leben | Life |
| Das Leder, Die Leder | Leather |
| Das Leiden, Die Leiden | Suffering |
| Das Lenkrad, Die Lenkräder | Steering Wheel |
| Das Lettisch | Latvian (language) |
| Das Licht, Die Lichter | Light |
| Das Lieblingsessen, Die Lieblingsspeisen | Favorite Food |

| German | English |
|--------|---------|
| Das Lied, Die Lieder | Song |
| Das Litauisch | Lithuanian (language) |
| Das Loch, Die Löcher | Hole |
| Das Lorbeerblatt | Bay Leaf |
| Das Los, Die Lose | Lot (situation, the what's-going-on) |
| Das Mädchen, Die Mädchen | Girl |
| Das Make-up | Makeup Foundation |
| Das Mal, Die Male | Timepoint |
| Das Mandarin | Mandarin (language) |
| Das Märchen, Die Märchen | Fairy Tale |
| Das Maultier, Die Maultiere | Mule |
| Das Maximum, Die Maxima | Maximum |
| Das Medikament, Die Medikamenten | Medication, Drug, Medicine |
| Das Meer, Die Meere | Sea |
| Das Meerschweinchen, Die Meerschweinchen | Guinea Pig |
| Das Mehl, Die Mehle | Flour |
| Das Merkmal, Die Merkmale | Feature |
| Das Messer, Die Messer | Knife |
| Das Metall, Die Metalle | Metal |
| Das Mikrofon, Die Mikrofone | Microphone |
| Das Mitglied, Die Mitglieder | Member |
| Das Mittagessen, Die Mittagessen | Lunch |
| Das Mittelfeld, Die Mittelfelder | Midfield |
| Das Modell, Die Modelle | Model (person or thing, such as a fashion model or airplane model) |
| Das Molekül, Die Moleküle | Molecule |
| Das Mondlicht | Moonlight (from the moon) |
| Das Museum, Die Museen | Museum |
| Das Muster, Die Muster | Pattern |
| Das Nachrichtenportal, Die Nachrichtenportale | News Portal |
| Das Nashorn, Die Nashörner | Rhinoceros |
| Das Nebenfach, Die Nebenfächer | Minor (college) |
| Das Neon | Neon |
| Das Nest, Die Nester | Nest |
| Das Neutron, Die Neutronen | Neutron |
| Das Nichts | Nothing |
| Das Nickerchen, Die Nickerchen | Nap, Snooze |
| Das Niederländisch | Dutch (language) |
| Das Norwegisch | Norwegian (language) |
| Das Nudelholz, Die Nudelhölzer | Rolling Pin |
| Das Nummernschild, Die Nummernschilder | License Plate |

| German | English |
|---|---|
| Das Objekt, Die Objekte | Object (grammar, astronomy) |
| Das Obst | Fruit (the plant seed) |
| Das Ohr, Die Ohren | Ear |
| Das Öl, Die Öle | Oil |
| Das Olivenöl, Die Olivenöle | Olive Oil |
| Das Opfer, Die Opfer | Victim |
| Das Optikergeschäft, Die Optikergeschäfte | Eyeglass Store |
| Das Orange, Die Orange | Orange (color) |
| Das Paar, Die Paare | Pair |
| Das Paniermehl, Die Paniermehle | Breading, Bread Crumbs |
| Das Papier, Die Papiere | Paper |
| Das Paradies, Die Paradiese | Paradise |
| Das Paschtunisch | Pashto (language) |
| Das Persisch | Persian (language) |
| Das Personal | Staff |
| Das Pfeffer, Die Pfeffer | Pepper |
| Das Pferd, Die Pferde | Horse |
| Das Pflegeheim, Die Pflegeheime | Nursing Home |
| Das Pfund, Die Pfunde | Pound (British currency) |
| Das Picknick, Die Picknicks | Picnic |
| Das Pils, Die Pils | Pilsner |
| Das Polnisch | Polish (language) |
| Das Polygon, Die Polygone | Polygon |
| Das Popcorn | Popcorn |
| Das Portal, Die Portale | Portal |
| Das Portugiesisch | Portuguese (language) |
| Das Postamt, Die Postämter | Post Office |
| Das Postfach, Die Postfächer | Mailbox |
| Das Problem, Die Probleme | Problem |
| Das Produkt, Die Produkte | Product (math) |
| Das Proton, Die Protonen | Proton |
| Das Prozent, Die Prozente | Percent |
| Das Publikum | Public |
| Das Quadrat, Die Quadräte | Square |
| Das Rad, Die Räder | Wheel |
| Das Radio, Die Radios | Radio |
| Das Radrennen, Die Radrennen | Bike Race |
| Das Rathaus, Die Rathäuser | City Hall |
| Das Recht, Die Rechte | Right |
| Das Rechteck, Die Rechtecke | Rectangle |
| Das Regal, Die Regale | Shelf |
| Das Regeln, Die Regeln | Policy |
| Das Regeln, Die Regeln | Regulation |

| German | English |
| --- | --- |
| Das Rennen, Die Rennen | Race (sports) |
| Das Restaurant, Die Restaurants | Restaurant |
| Das Rezept, Die Rezepte | Recipe |
| Das Rindfleisch | Beef |
| Das Ringbuch, Die Ringbücher | Ringed Binder |
| Das Risk, Die Risken | Risk |
| Das Röntgen | X-Ray |
| Das Rote Kreuz | Red Cross |
| Das Ruderboot, Die Ruderboote | Rowboat |
| Das Rührei, Die Rühreier | Scrambled Egg |
| Das Rumänisch | Romanian (language) |
| Das Russisch | Russian (language) |
| Das Sakko, Die Sakkos | Sport Coat |
| Das Sakrament, Die Sakramente | Sacrament |
| Das Salz, Die Salze | Salt |
| Das Saxaphon, Die Saxaphone | Saxophone |
| Das Schach, Die Schachspiele | Chess |
| Das Schalentier, Die Schalentiere | Shellfish |
| Das Schicksal, Die Schicksale | Destiny |
| Das Schiff, Die Schiffe | Ship |
| Das Schild, Die Schilder (different from Der Schild) | Sign, Plate (road) |
| Das Schlafzimmer, Die Schlafzimmer | Bedroom |
| Das Schnitzel, Die Schnitzel | Cutlet, Schnitzel (cooking) |
| Das Schwedisch | Swedish (language) |
| Das Schwein, Die Schweine | Pig |
| Das Schweinefleisch | Pork |
| Das Schwert, Die Schwerter | Sword |
| Das Schwimmbad, Die Schwimmbäder | Swimming Pool |
| Das Schwimmbecken, Die Pools | Pool |
| Das Semester, Die Semester | Semester |
| Das Serbisch | Serbian (language) |
| Das Silber, Die Silber | Silver |
| Das Sofa, Die Sofas | Couch |
| Das Spiegelbild, Die Spiegelbilder | Reflection, Mirror Image |
| Das Spiel, Die Spiele | Game |
| Das Spielzeug, Die Spielzeuge | Toy |
| Das Steak, Die Steaks | Steak |
| Das Sternzeichen, Die Sternzeichen | Zodiac Sign |
| Das Stiefkind, Die Stiefkinder | Stepchild |
| Das Stoppschild, Die Stoppschilder | Stop Sign |
| Das Stroh | Straw |
| Das Stück, Die Stücke | Piece |

| German | English |
|---|---|
| Das Studentenwohnheim, Die Studentenwohnheime | Dorm (for students) |
| Das Studio, Die Studios | Studio |
| Das Substantiv, Die Substantive | Noun |
| Das Surfbrett, Die Surfbretter | Surfboard |
| Das Swahili | Swahili (language) |
| Das System, Die Systems | System |
| Das Szenario, Die Szenarien | Scenario |
| Das Tabellenwerk, Die Tabellenwerke | Table (data) |
| Das Tafelsilber | Silverware |
| Das Tagalog | Tagalog (language) |
| Das Taschentuch, Die Taschentücher | Handkerchief |
| Das Taufbecken, Die Taufbecken | Baptismal Font |
| Das Taxi, Die Taxis | Taxi |
| Das Team, Die Teams | Team |
| Das Telefon, Die Telefone | Phone |
| Das Tempo, Die Tempi, Die Tempos | Tempo |
| Das Tennis | Tennis |
| Das Tennisspiel, Die Tennisspiele | Tennis Match |
| Das Termingeschäft, Die Termingeschäfte | Futures (financial) |
| Das Theater, Die Theater | Theater |
| Das Thema, Die Themen | Topic |
| Das Ticket, Die Tickets | Ticket |
| Das Tier, Die Tiere | Animal |
| Das Tor, Die Tore | Gate |
| Das Tor, Die Tore | Goal (as in scoring a goal) |
| Das Tornetz, Die Tornetze | Soccer Net |
| Das Treffe, Die Treffen | Meeting |
| Das Trikot, Die Trikots | Jersey (soccer) |
| Das Tschechisch | Czech (language) |
| Das Türkisch | Turkish (language) |
| Das Ukrainisch | Ukrainian (language) |
| Das Unbekannte, Die Unbekannten | Unknown (the unknown, not a person) |
| Das Ungarisch | Hungarian (language) |
| Das Unternehmen, Die Unternehmen | Venture, Undertaking (economic) |
| Das Urteil, Die Urteile | Judgement |
| Das Veränderung, Die Veränderungen | Transformation |
| Das Verb, Die Verben | Verb |
| Das Verbot, Die Verbote | Ban |
| Das Verfahren, Die Verfahren | Procedure, Method |
| Das Vergnügen, Die Vergnügen | Enjoyment |
| Das Verhältnis, Die Verhältnisse | Ratio, Proportion |
| Das Verlangen, Die Verlangen | Craving |

| German | English |
| --- | --- |
| Das Verlängerungskabel, Die Verlängerungskabel | Extension Cord |
| Das Versehen, Die Versehen | Oversight, Mistake |
| Das Verständnis, Die Verständnisse | Understanding, Insight |
| Das Video, Die Videos | Video |
| Das Vieh | Cattle |
| Das Vieh | Livestock |
| Das Virus, Die Viren | Virus |
| Das Volk, Die Völker | Folk, Public |
| Das Volk, Die Völker | People |
| Das Vortstellungsgespräch, Die Vortstellungsgespräche | Interview |
| Das Wachs, Die Wachse | Wax |
| Das Wachstum | Growth |
| Das Waldhorn, Die Waldhörner | French Horn |
| Das Walisisch | Welsh (language) |
| Das Wandern, Die Wanderungen | Hike |
| Das Wasser, Die Wasser | Water |
| Das Weihnachten, Die Weihnachten (usually no article) | Christmas |
| Das Weizenbier, Die Weizenbiere | Wheat Beer |
| Das Wetter | Weather |
| Das Wirtshaus, Die Wirtshäuser | Tavern |
| Das Wissen | Knowledge |
| Das Wochenende, Die Wochenenden | Weekend |
| Das Wort, Die Wörter | Word |
| Das Wörterbuch, Die Wörterbücher | Dictionary |
| Das Yoga | Yoga |
| Das Zebra, Die Zebras | Zebra |
| Das Zentrum, Die Zentren | Center |
| Das Zeug, Die Stoffe | Stuff |
| Das Zeugnis, Die Zeugnisse | Report |
| Das Ziel, Die Ziele | Goal (as in working toward a goal) |
| Das Zimmer, Die Zimmer | Room |
| Das Zuhause | Home |

# 13

## ENGLISH TO GERMAN

| English | German |
|---|---|
| Abandonment | Die Verlassenheit |
| Abbey | Die Abtei, Die Abteien |
| Abdomen | Der Bauch, Die Bäuche |
| Ability, Skill | Die Fähigkeit, Die Fähigkeiten |
| Abortion | Die Abtreibung, Die Abtreibungen |
| Abstinence | Die Enthaltsamkeit |
| Abundance | Die Fülle |
| Abuse | Die Beschimpfung, Die Beschimpfungen |
| Academic Advisor | Der Studienberater, Die Studienberater; Die Studienberatin, Die Studienberatinnen |
| Accommodation, Housing | Die Unterkunft, Die Unterkünfte |
| Accomplice | Der Mittäter, Die Mittäter; Die Mittäterin, Die Mittäterinnen |
| Accomplishment | Die Leistung, Die Leistungen |
| Account | Das Konto, Die Konten |
| Accuracy | Die Genauigkeit, Die Genauigkeiten |
| Accusation | Die Anklage, Die Anklagen |
| Accused | Der Angeklagte, Die Angeklagten; Die Angeklagten, Die Angeklagtenin |
| Achievement, Attainment | Die Errungenschaft, Die Errungenschäfte |
| Acquisition, Procurement | Die Beschaffung, Die Beschaffungen |
| Acrylic Paint | Die Acrylfarbe, Die Acrylfarben |
| Action | Die Aktion, Die Aktionen |
| Action | Das Handeln |
| Activism | Der Aktivismus |
| Activity | Die Aktivität, Die Aktivitäten |
| Actor, Actress | Der Schauspieler, Die Schauspieler; Die Schauspielerin, Die Schauspielerinnen |
| Address | Die Adresse, Die Adressen |

| English | German |
|---------|--------|
| Adhesive, Glue | Der Klebstoff, Die Klebstoffe |
| Adjective | Das Adjektiv, Die Adjektive |
| Administration | Die Verwaltungen, Die Verwaltungen |
| Adult | Der Ewachsene, Die Erwachsenen |
| Advantage | Der Vorteil, Die Vorteile |
| Adventure | Das Abenteuer, Die Abenteuer |
| Advertisement | Die Anzeige, Die Anzeigen |
| Advisor | Der Berater, Die Berater; Die Beaterin, Die Beaterinnen |
| Affair, Issue | Die Angelegenheit, Die Angelegenheiten |
| Affiliation, Party, Club | Die Zugehörigkeit, Die Zugehörigkeiten |
| Aftermath | Die Folge, Die Folgen |
| Afternoon | Der Nachmittag, Die Nachmittage |
| Age | Das Alte, Die Alte |
| Agency | Die Agentur, Die Agenturen |
| Agenda | Die Tagesordnung, Die Tagesordnungen |
| Agent | Der Agent, Die Agenten; Die Agentin, Die Agentinnen |
| Agent, Representative | Der Vertreter, Die Vertreterin |
| Agreement | Die Vereinbarung, Die Vereinbarungen |
| Air | Die Luft, Die Lüfte |
| Air Conditioner | Die Klimaanlage, Die Klimaanlagen |
| Air Force | Die Luftwaffe, Die Luftwaffen |
| Airfield | Der Flugplatz, Die Flugplätze |
| Airplane | Das Flugzeug, Die Flugzeuge |
| Airport | Der Flughafen, Die Flughäfen |
| Airport Terminal | Das Flughafenterminal, Die Flughafenterminals |
| Aisle (also course as in *three-course meal*) | Der Gang, Die Gänge |
| Alarm Clock | Der Wecker, Die Wecker |
| Algebra | Die Algebra, Die Algeberen |
| Algorithm | Der Algorithmus, Die Algorithmen |
| Allegations | Der Vorwurf, Die Vorwürfe |
| Allocate Credit | Die Vergabe, Die Vergaben |
| Almond | Die Mandel, Die Mandeln |
| Alphabet | Das Alphabet, Die Alphabete |
| Alps | Die Alpen |
| Altitude | Die Höhenlage, Die Höhenlagen |
| Alto | Der Altist, Die Altisten; Die Altistin, Die Altistinnen |
| Ambulance | Der Krankenwagen, Die Krankenwagen |
| Ammunition | Die Munition, Die Munitionen |
| Amount | Der Betrag, Die Beträge |
| Amount, Quantity | Die Menge, Die Mengen |

| English | German |
|---|---|
| Amplifier | Der Verstärker, Die Verstärker |
| Anarchist | Der Anarchist, Die Anarchisten; Die Anarchistin, Die Anarchistinnen |
| Anarchy | Der Anarchismus |
| Anatomy | Die Anatomie, Die Anatomien |
| Ancestor | Der Ahne, Die Ahnen; Die Ahnin, Die Ahninnen |
| Ancestor | Der Vorfahre, Die Vorfahren |
| Anchor | Der Anker, Die Anker |
| Anger | Der Zorn |
| Angle | Der Winkel, Die Winkel |
| Animal | Das Tier, Die Tiere |
| Animal Rights Activist | Der Tierschützer, Die Tierschützer; Die Tierschützerin, Die Tierschützerinnen |
| Ankle | Der Knöchel, Die Knöchel |
| Announcement | Die Ankündigung, Die Ankündigungen |
| Annoyance | Das Ärgernis, Die Ärgernisse |
| Answer | Die Antwort, Die Antworten |
| Ant | Die Ameise, Die Ameisen |
| Antique | Die Antiquität, Die Antiquitäten |
| Antiquity | Das Altertum |
| Apartment | Die Wohnung, Die Wohnungen |
| Appearance | Das Aussehen |
| Apple | Der Apfel, Die Äpfel |
| Apple Juice | Der Apfelsaft, Die Apfelsäfte |
| Applicant | Der Bewerber, Die Bewerber; Die Bewerberin, Die Bewerberinnen |
| Application, Proposal, a Motion | Der Antrag, Die Anträge |
| Approach | Der Anflug, Die Anflüge |
| April | Der April |
| Aquarius | Der Wassermann, Die Wassermänner |
| Arabic (language) | Das Arabisch |
| Aramaic (language) | Das Aramäisch |
| Archbishop | Der Erzbischof, Die Erzbischöfe |
| Area (larger) | Das Gebiet, Die Gebiete |
| Area (living) | Die Gegend, Die Gegenden |
| Area (smaller) | Der Bereich, Die Bereiche |
| Argument (statement to convince) | Das Argument, Die Argumente |
| Argument, Quarrel | Die Auseinandersetzung, Die Auseinandersetzungen |
| Aries | Der Widder, Die Widder |
| Arm | Der Arm, Die Arme |
| Armchair | Der Sessel, Die Sessel |

| English | German |
|---|---|
| Armenian (language) | Das Armenisch |
| Army | Die Armee, Die Armeen |
| Arrangement, Design | Die Gestaltung, Die Gestaltungen |
| Arrogance | Die Arroganz |
| Art | Die Kunst, Die Künste |
| Arthropod (shrimp, crabs, lobsters) | Der Gliederflüßler, Die Gliederflüßler |
| Assault, Offensive | Der Angriff, Die Angriffe |
| Assembly, Gathering | Die Versammlung, Die Versammlungen |
| Association (club) | Der Verein, Die Vereine |
| Astronomy | Die Astronomie |
| Astronomy | Die Himmelskunde |
| Astronomy | Die Sternkunde |
| Atheism | Der Atheismus |
| Atheist | Der Atheist, Die Atheisten; Die Atheistin, Die Atheistinnen |
| Athletic Field, Arena | Der Sportplatz, Die Sportplätze |
| Athletic Shoe | Der Sportschuh, Die Sportschuhe |
| Athletics | Der Sport |
| Atlantic | Der Atlantik |
| ATM | Der Geldautomat, Die Geldautomaten |
| Atom | Das Atom, Die Atome |
| Atomic Bomb | Die Atombombe, Die Atombomben |
| Attack | Der Anschlag, Die Anschläge |
| Attention (focus) | Die Aufmerksamkeit, Die Aufmerksamkeiten |
| Attitude | Die Einstellung, Die Einstellungen |
| Audience | Die Zuhörer (different from Der Zuhörer) |
| August | Der August |
| Aunt | Die Tante, Die Tanten |
| Author | Der Autor, Die Autoren; Die Autorin, Die Autorinnen |
| Autumn | Der Herbst, Die Herbste |
| Award (contract), Allocate | Die Vergabe, Die Vergaben |
| Awareness | Die Bewusstsein, Die Bewusstseine |
| Baby | Das Baby, Die Babys |
| Bachelor | Der Junggeselle, Die Junggesellen |
| Bachelor's Degree | Der Bakkalaureus, Die Bakkalaurei |
| Back | Der Rücken, Die Rücken |
| Background | Der Hintergrund, Die Hintergründe |
| Backseat | Der Rücksitz, Die Rücksitze |
| Bacon | Der Speck |
| Bacteria | Die Bakterien |
| Bag | Der Beutel, Die Taschen |
| Baggage Claim | Die Gepäckausgabe, Die Gepäckausgaben |

| English | German |
|---------|--------|
| Baking Sheet | Das Backblech, Die Backbleche |
| Balcony | Der Balkon, Die Balkone |
| Ball | Der Ball, Die Bälle |
| Ban | Das Verbot, Die Verbote |
| Banana | Die Banane, Die Bananen |
| Band | Die Band, Die Bands |
| Band, Brass | Die Blaskapelle, Die Blasskapellen |
| Bank | Die Bank, Die Banken |
| Baptism | Die Taufe, Die Taufen |
| Baptismal Font | Das Taufbecken, Die Taufbecken |
| Bar | Die Bar, Die Bars |
| Barbecue Grill | Der Grill, Die Grills |
| Barracks | Die Kaserne, Die Kasernen |
| Baseball | Der Baseball, Die Baseballs |
| Basketball | Der Basketball, Die Basketbälle |
| Basketball | Der Korbball, Die Korbbälle |
| Bass (fish) | Der Barsch, Die Barsche |
| Bass (instrument) | Der Bass, Die Bässe |
| Bass (person) | Der Bassist, Die Bassisten; Die Bassistin, Die Bassistinnen |
| Bat | Die Fledermaus, Die Fledermäuse |
| Bathroom | Das Bad, Die Badezimmer |
| Bathtub | Die Badewanne, Die Badewannen |
| Battle | Die Schlacht, Die Schlachten |
| Bay | Die Bucht, Die Buchten |
| Bay Leaf | Das Lorbeerblatt |
| Beach | Der Strand, Die Strände |
| Beachguard | Die Strandwache, Die Strandwachen |
| Beak, birds | Der Schnabel, Die Schnäbel |
| Bean | Die Bohne, Die Bohnen |
| Beat music | Der Beat |
| Beauty | Die Schönheit, Die Schönheiten |
| Bed | Das Bett, Die Betten |
| Bedroom | Das Schlafzimmer, Die Schlafzimmer |
| Bee | Die Biene, Die Bienen |
| Beef | Das Rindfleisch |
| Beer | Das Bier, Die Biere |
| Beetle | Der Käfer, Die Käfer |
| Beginner | Der Anfänger, Die Anfänger |
| Beginning | Der Anfange, Die Anfänge |
| Belief | Der Glaube, Die Glauben |
| Believer | Der Gläubige, Die Gläubigen |
| Bell | Die Glocke, Die Glocken |
| Belt | Der Gürtel, Die Gurtel |

| English | German |
|---------|--------|
| Benefit | Der Nutzen, Die Nutzen |
| Betrayal, Treason | Der Verrat |
| Beverage, Drink | Das Getränk, Die Getränke |
| Bible | Die Bibel, Die Bibeln |
| Bicycle | Das Fahrrad, Die Fahrräder |
| Bike Race | Das Radrennen, Die Radrennen |
| Bill | Die Rechnung, Die Rechnungen |
| Billions | Die Milliarden |
| Biology | Die Biologie |
| Bird | Der Vogel, Die Vögel |
| Bishop | Der Bischof, Die Bischöfe |
| Bitcoin | Der Bitcoin |
| Blade | Die Klinge, Die Klingen |
| Blanket | Die Decke, Die Decken |
| Blessing | Der Segen, Die Segen (plural is rare) |
| Block | Der Block, Die Blöcke |
| Blood | Das Blut, Die Blut |
| Blood Pressure | Der Blutdruck, Die Blutdrücke |
| Blood Sausage | Die Blutwurst, Die Blutwürste |
| Blouse | Die Bluse, Die Blusen |
| Blueberry | Die Heidelbeer, Die Heidelbeeren |
| Board (or type of table, flat piece) | Die Tafel, Die Tafeln |
| Boat | Das Boot, Die Boote |
| Bob (hairstyle) | Die Bob, Die Bobs |
| Body | Der Körper, Die Körper |
| Bombardment | Die Beschießung, Die Beschießungen |
| Bombardment | Das Bombardment, Die Bombardments |
| Bombing | Die Bombardierung, Die Bombardierungen |
| Bone | Der Knochen, Die Knochen |
| Bonus | Der Bonus, Die Bonus |
| Book | Das Buch, Die Bücher |
| Bookshelf | Das Buchregale, Die Bücherregale |
| Bookstore | Die Buchhandlung, Die Buchhandlungen |
| Boot (shoe) | Der Stiefel, Die Stiefel |
| Boss | Der Chef, Die Chefs; Die Chefin, Die Chefinnen |
| Bottle | Die Flasche, Die Flaschen |
| Bottom | Der Boden, Die Böden |
| Bourbon | Der Bourbon, Die Bourbons |
| Bowl | Die Schale, Die Schalen |
| Box | Die Schachtel, Die Schachteln |
| Box, Chest | Der Kasten, Die Kästen |
| Boy | Der Knabe, Die Knaben |
| Bra | Der Büstenhalter, Die Büstenhalter (BH) |

| English | German |
|---------|--------|
| Brain | Das Gehirn, Die Gehirne |
| Brake | Die Bremse, Die Bremsen |
| Brake Light | Das Bremslicht, Die Bremslichter |
| Branch (of an organization) | Die Niederlassung, Die Niederlassungen |
| Branch, tree | Der Ast, Die Äste |
| Bratwurst | Die Bratwurst, Die Bratwürste |
| Bread | Das Brot, Die Brote |
| Breading, Bread Crumbs | Das Paniermehl, Die Paniermehle |
| Breakfast | Das Frühstück, Die Frühstücke |
| Breast | Die Brust, Die Brüste |
| Breath | Der Atem, Die Atem |
| Bride | Die Braut, Die Bräute |
| Bridegroom | Der Bräutigam, Die Bräutigams |
| Bridge | Die Brücke, Die Brücken |
| Broccoli | Der Brokkoli, Die Brokkolis |
| Bronze Medal | Die Bronzemedaille, Die Bronzemedaillen |
| Broom | Der Besen, Die Besen |
| Brother | Der Bruder, Die Brüder |
| Bubble | Die Blase, Die Blasen |
| Building | Das Gebäude, Die Gebäude |
| Bulgarian (language) | Das Bulgarisch |
| Bulk, Gross | Das Gros, Die Grosse |
| Bullet | Die Kugel, Die Kugeln |
| Bus | Der Bus, Die Busse |
| Bus stop | Die Haltestelle, Die Haltestellen |
| Butter | Die Butter |
| Button | Der Knopf, Die Knöpfe |
| Buyer | Der Käufer, Die Käufer; Die Käuferin, Die Käuferinnen |
| Café | Das Café, Die Cafés |
| Calculation | Das Kalkül, Die Kalküle |
| Calculator | Der Rechner, Die Rechner |
| Call | Der Anruf, Die Anrufe |
| Camera | Die Kamera, Die Kameras |
| Camouflage (clothing) | Die Camoflauge, Die Camoflaugen |
| Camouflage (cover, to hide) | Die Tarnung, Die Tarnungen |
| Camp | Das Lager, Die Lager |
| Cancel (such as at an ATM) | Der Abbruch, Die Abbrüche |
| Cancer | Der Krebs, Die Krebse |
| Candidate | Der Bewerber, Die Bewerber; Die Bewerberin, Die Bewerberinnen |
| Candidate | Der Kandidat, Die Kandidaten; Die Kandidatin, Die Kandidatinnen |
| Candle | Die Kerze, Die Kerzen |

| English | German |
|---------|--------|
| Candy | Das Bonbon, Die Bonbons |
| Canned Goods | Die Konserve, Die Konserven |
| Canoe | Das Kanu, Die Kanus |
| Canteen (camping) | Die Feldflasche, Die Feldflaschen |
| Canteen (snack bar) | Die Kantine, Die Kantinen |
| Cape | Das Kap, Die Kaps |
| Capital | Die Hauptstadt, Die Hauptstädte |
| Capital | Das Kapital |
| Capricorn | Der Steinbock, Die Steinböcke |
| Captain | Der Kapitän, Die Kapitäne, Die Kapitänin, Die Kapitäninnen |
| Car | Das Auto, Die Autos |
| Car Hood | Die Motorhaube, Die Motorhauben |
| Car Race | Das Autorennen, Die Autorennen |
| Car Trunk | Der Kofferraum, Die Kofferräume |
| Card | Die Karte, Die Karten |
| Cardinal | Der Kardinal, Die Kardinäle |
| Care | Die Pflege |
| Career | Der Beruf, Die Berufe |
| Caregiver | Der Pfleger, Die Pfleger; Die Pflegerin, Die Pflegerinnen |
| Carrot | Die Karotte, Die Karotten |
| Case (large box) | Die Kiste, Die Kisten |
| Cash | Das Bargeld |
| Cash Register | Die Kasse, Die Kassen |
| Cassette | Die Kassette, Die Kassetten |
| Castle, Stronghold, Fortress | Die Burg, Die Burgen |
| Cat | Die Katze, Die Katzen |
| Catastrophe | Die Katastrophe, Die Katasrophen |
| Catch (of the day) | Der Fing, Die Fänge |
| Cattle | Das Vieh |
| Cauliflower | Der Blumenkohl, Die Blumenkohle |
| Cause | Die Ursache, Die Ursachen |
| Ceiling | Die Decke, Die Decken |
| Celebration, Party | Die Feier, Die Feieren |
| Celery | Der Sellerie, Die Sellerie |
| Cell | Die Zelle, Die Zellen |
| Cello | Das Cello, Die Cellos |
| Cellphone | Das Handy, Die Handys |
| Center | Das Zentrum, Die Zentren |
| Chain | Die Kette, Die Ketten |
| Chair | Der Stuhl, Die Stühle |
| Chairperson | Der Vorsitzende, Die Vorsitzenden; Die Vorsitzende, Die Vorsitzenden |

| English | German |
|---------|--------|
| Chalk | Die Kreide |
| Challenge | Die Herausforderung, Die Herausforderungen |
| Championship | Die Meisterschaft, Die Meisterschaften |
| Chance | Die Chance, Die Chancen |
| Change (in weather, etc.) | Der Wechsel, Die Wechsel |
| Chapter | Das Kapitel, Die Kapitel |
| Character | Der Charakter, Die Charaktere |
| Charity (organization) | Die Wohltätigkeitsorganisation, Die Wohltätigkeitsorganisationen |
| Charity (wholesome deeds) | Die Wohltätigkeit, Die Wohltätigkeiten |
| Check | Der Scheck, Die Schecks |
| Check | Die Rechnung, Die Rechnungen |
| Cheek | Die Wange, Die Wangen |
| Chemistry | Die Chemie |
| Cherry | Die Kirsche, Die Kirschen |
| Chess | Das Schach, Die Schachspiele |
| Chest (biology) | Die Brust, Die Truhen |
| Chestnut | Die Kastanie, Die Kastanien |
| Chick, Baby Chicken | Das Küken, Die Küken |
| Chicken | Das Huhn, Die Hühner |
| Chickpea | Der Kichererbsen, Die Kichererbsen |
| Child | Das Kind, Die Kinder |
| Children's Book | Das Kinderbuch, Die Kinderbüche |
| Chimes | Das Glockenspiel, Die Glockenspiele |
| Chin | Das Kinn, Die Kinne |
| Chinese (language) | Das Chinesisch |
| Chocolate | Die Schokolade, Die Schokoladen |
| Chocolate Coating | Die Kuvertüre, Die Kuvertüren |
| Choice | Die Auswahl, Die Auswahlen |
| Choice (election, also what you choose) | Die Wahl, Die Wahlen |
| Choir | Der Chor, Die Chöre |
| Chores, Housework | Die Hausarbeit, Die Hausarbeiten |
| Christian | Der Christ, Die Christen; Die Christin, Die Christinnen |
| Christianity | Die Christentum |
| Christmas | Das Weihnachten, Die Weihnachten (usually no article) |
| Church | Die Kirche, Die Kirchen |
| Cigar | Die Zigarre, Die Zigarren |
| Cigarette | Die Zigarrette, Die Zigarretten |
| Cigarette Machine | Der Zigarrettenautomat, Die Zigarrettenautomaten |
| Cilantro | Der Koriander |

| English | German |
|---|---|
| Cinema | Das Kino, Die Kinos |
| Cinnamon | Der Zimt |
| Circle | Der Kreis, Die Kreise |
| Circus | Der Zirkus, Die Zirkusse |
| Citizen | Der Bürger, Die Bürger; Die Bürgerin, Die Bürgerinnen |
| City | Die Stadt, Die Städte |
| City Hall | Das Rathaus, Die Rathäuser |
| Clam | Die Muschel, Die Muscheln |
| Clarinet | Die Klarinette, Die Klarinetten |
| Class | Die Klasse, Die Klassen |
| Class Struggle | Der Klassenkampf, Die Klassenkämpfe |
| Class Warfare | Der Klassenkrieg, Die Klassenkriege |
| Classmate | Der Klassenkamerad, Die Klassenkameraden; Die Klassenkameradin, Die Klassenkameradinnen |
| Classroom | Das Klassenzimmer, Die Klassenzimmer |
| Claw, Hook (as in hand) | Der Krall, Die Krallen |
| Climate | Das Klima, Die Klimas |
| Climate Protection | Der Klimaschutz |
| Cloak | Der Umhang, Die Umhänge |
| Clock | Die Uhr, Die Uhren |
| Clothes | no singular, Die Kleider |
| Clothes, Gear | no singular, Die Klamotten |
| Cloud | Die Wolke, Die Wolken |
| Club | Der Klub, Die Klubs |
| Coach (sports) | Der Trainer, Die Trainer; Die Trainerin, Die Trainerinnen |
| Coast | Die Küste, Die Küsten |
| Coaster | Der Bierdeckel, Die Bierdeckel |
| Coat | Der Mantel, Die Mäntel |
| Cockroach | Die Kakerlake, Die Kakerlaken |
| Cod | Der Dorsch |
| Cod | Der Kabeljau |
| Coffee | Der Kaffee, Die Kaffee |
| Coffee Table | Der Couchtisch, Die Couchtische |
| Coffee Vending Machine | Der Kaffeeautomat, Die Kaffeeutomaten |
| Cognac | Der Cognac, Die Cognacs |
| Coincidence, Chance | Der Zufall, Die Zufälle |
| Coins | Die Münze, Die Münzen |
| Coke Machine, Soda Machine | Der Cola-Automat, Die Cola-Automaten |
| Cold | Die Erkältung, Die Erkältungen |
| Colleague | Der Kollege, Die Kollegen |
| College | Das College, Die Colleges |

| English | German |
|---|---|
| Color | Die Farbe, Die Farben |
| Comedy | Die Komödie, Die Komödien |
| Commander | Der Kommandant, Die Kommandanten |
| Commandment | Das Gebot, Die Gebote |
| Commitment | Die Verpflichtung, Die Verpflichtungen |
| Committee | Der Ausschuss, Die Ausschüsse |
| Communication, Notice | Die Mitteilung, Die Mitteilungen |
| Communion | Das Abendmahl, Die Kommunion |
| Communism | Der Komminismus |
| Communist | Der Kommunist, Die Kommunisten; Die Kommunistin, Die Kommunistinnen |
| Community | Die Gemeinschaft, Die Gemeinschaften |
| Companion, Comrade | Der Genosse, Die Genossen; Die Genossin, Die Genossinnen |
| Compartment | Das Fach, Die Fäche |
| Competence | Die Kompetenz, Die Kompetenzen |
| Competition | Der Wettbewerb, Die Wettbewerbe |
| Competitiveness | Die Wettbewerbsfähigkeit, Die Wettbewerbsfähigkeiten |
| Competitor | Der Mitbewerber, Die Mitbewerber; Die Mitbewerberin, Die Mitbewerberinnen |
| Complaint | Die Beschwerde, Die Beschwerden |
| Computer (electronic) | Der Computer, Die Computer |
| Computer (someone or something that computes) | Der Rechner, Die Rechner |
| Computer Storage | Der Speicherplatz, Die Speicherplätze |
| Comrade | Der Kamerad, Die Kameraden; Die Kameradin, Die Kameradinnen |
| Concern, Issue | Das Anliegen, Die Anliegen |
| Concert | Das Konzert, Die Konzerte |
| Condition (appearance) | Der Zustand, Die Zustände |
| Condition (of a contract) | Die Bedingung, Die Bedingungen |
| Confirmation, Enter at an ATM | Die Bestätigung, Die Bestätigungen |
| Confusion | Die Verwirrung, Die Verwirrungen |
| Congress | Der Kongress, Die Kongresse |
| Conquest | Die Eroberung, Die Eroberungen |
| Consciousness | Das Bewusstsein |
| Consent, Agreement | Die Zustimmung, Die Zustimmungen |
| Consequence | Die Folge, Die Folgen |
| Consumer | Der Verbraucher, Die Verbraucher; Die Verbraucherin, Die Verbraucherinnen |
| Contamination | Die Verschmutzung, Die Verschmutzungen |
| Context | Der Zusammenhang, Die Zusammenhänge |

| English | German |
|---------|--------|
| Contract | Der Vertrag, Die Verträge |
| Contractions, Labor Pains | no singular, Die Wehen |
| Contribution | Der Beitrag, Die Beiträge |
| Control | Die Kontrolle, Die Steuerelemente |
| Conversation (casual) | Die Unterhaltung, Die Unterhaltungen |
| Conversation (not personal) | Das Gespräch, Die Gespräche |
| Conviction (convinced) | Die Überzeugung, Die Überzeugungen |
| Cooperation | Die Zusammenarbeit |
| Copper | Das Kupfer |
| Corn | Der Mais |
| Corn Starch (thickener) | Die Speisestärke |
| Corner | Die Ecke, Die Ecken |
| Correction | Die Korrektur, Die Korrekturen |
| Corrective Action, Counter Measures | Die Gegenmaßnahmen, Die Gegenmaßnahmen |
| Cosmetic Store | Die Parfümerie, Die Parfümerien |
| Cost | Die Kosten, Die Kosten |
| Couch | Das Couch, Die Couchen |
| Couch | Das Sofa, Die Sofas |
| Cough | Der Husten |
| Council, Guidance | Der Rat, Die Räte |
| Counter (person who counts) | Der Zähler, Die Zähler; Die Zählerin, Die Zählerinnen |
| Countertop | Die Arbeitsplatte, Die Arbeitsplatten |
| Counterweight | Das Gegengewicht, Die Gegengewichte |
| Country | Das Land, Die Länder |
| Coup | Der Streich, Die Streiche |
| Couple | Das Ehepaar, Die Paare |
| Coupon | Das Gutschein, Die Gutscheine |
| Course | Der Kurs, Die Kurse |
| Court | Das Gericht, Die Gerichte |
| Cousin | Der Cousin, Die Cousinen |
| Cow | Die Kuh, Die Kühe |
| Co-worker (worker in a group) | Der Mitarbeiter, Die Mitarbeiter; Die Mitarbeiterin, Die Mitarbeiterinnen |
| Crab | Die Krabbe, Die Krabben |
| Crab (classification) | Der Krebs, Die Krebse (Some *Krebse* are not crabs.) |
| Crab Claw | Die Krabbenschere, Die Krabbenscheren |
| Cracker | Der Knacker, Die Knacker |
| Craving | Das Verlangen, Die Verlangen |
| Creation (as in of the world, ex nihilo) | Die Schöpfung, Die Schöpfungen |

| English | German |
|---|---|
| Creation (establishment of, as in jobs) | Die Schaffung, Die Schaffungen |
| Creator | Der Schöpfer, Die Schöpfer; Die Schöpferin, Die Schöpferinnen |
| Crew | Die Besatzung, Die Besatzungen |
| Criminal | Der Verbrecher, Die Verbrecher; Die Verbrecherin, Die Verbrecherinnen |
| Cross | Das Kreuz, Die Kreuze |
| Crosswalk | Der Zebrastreifen, Die Zebrastreifen |
| Crossword Puzzle | Das Kreuzworträtsel, Die Kreuzworträtsel |
| Crowd | Die Menschenmasse, Die Menschenmassen |
| Cruise Ship | Der Kreuzfahrtschiff, Die Kreuzfahrtschiffe |
| Crustacean | Die Krustentiere, Die Krustentiere |
| Crutch | Die Krücke, Die Krücken |
| Crypto Currency | Die Kryptowährung, Die Kryptowährungen |
| Cube, Dice | Der Würfel, Die Würfel |
| Cubism | Der Kubismus |
| Cubist | Der Kubist, Die Kubisten; Die Kubistin, Die Kubistinnen |
| Cucumber | Die Gurke, Die Gurken |
| Culture | Die Kultur, Die Kulturen |
| Cup | Die Tasse, Die Tassen |
| Currency | Die Währung, Die Währungen |
| Current (electricity) | Der Strom, Die Ströme |
| Current (water) | Die Strömung, Die Strömungen |
| Curtain (not thin) | Der Vorhang, Die Vorhänge |
| Curtain (thin, allows light through) | Die Gardine, Die Gardinen |
| Customer | Der Kunde, Die Kunden |
| Customer Service | Der Kundendienst, Die Kundendienste |
| Cut (textile, film) | Der Schnitt, Die Schnitte |
| Cutlet, Schnitzel (cooking) | Das Schnitzel, Die Schnitzel |
| Cyclist | Der Radfahrer, Die Radfahrer; Die Radfahrerin, Die Radfahrerinnen |
| Czech (language) | Das Tschechisch |
| Dad | Der Papa, Die Papas |
| Damage | Der Schaden, Die Schäden |
| Dance | Der Tanz, Die Tänze |
| Danish (language) | Das Dänisch |
| Dark | Das Dunkel |
| Darkness | Die Dunkelheit, Die Dunkelheiten |
| Data | no singular, Die Daten |
| Database | Die Datenbank, Die Datenbanken |
| Date | Das Datum, Die Daten |

| English | German |
|---|---|
| Daughter | Die Tochter, Die Töchter |
| Day (entire) | Der Tag, Die Tagen |
| Deadline, Delivery, Levy | Die Abgabe, Die Abgaben |
| Deal, Agreement (political) | Das Abkommen, Die Abkommen |
| Death | Der Tod, Die Tode |
| Death | Der Todesfall, Die Todesfälle |
| Debt | Die Schuld, Die Schulden |
| Debt Limit | Die Schuldenbremse, Die Schuldenbremsen |
| Deceit, Ruse | Die List, Die Listen |
| December | Der Dezember |
| Decision | Die Entscheidung, Die Entscheidungen |
| Decision (group) | Der Beschluss, Die Beschlüsse |
| Deck | Die Terrasse, Die Terrassen |
| Decline | Der Niedergang |
| Decomposition, Disintegration | Die Zersetzung, Die Zersetzungen |
| Decree | Die Verordnung, Die Verordnungen |
| Deed, Act | Die Tat, Die Taten |
| Deeds | Die Tätigkeit, Die Tätigkeiten |
| Defense (sport), Resistance (as in WWII) | Die Abwehr |
| Definition | Die Definition, Die Definitionen |
| Delay | Die Verspätung, Die Verspätungen |
| Demand (claim) | Die Forderung, Die Forderungen |
| Demand (follow-up question) | Die Nachfrage, Die Nachfragen |
| Democracy | Die Demokratie, Die Demokratien |
| Democratic Republic of the Congo (DRC) | Die Demokratische Republik Kongo |
| Demolition | Der Abbruch, Die Abbrüche |
| Dentist | Der Zahnartzt, Die Zahnärtzten, Die Zahnärtztin, Die Zahnärtztinnen |
| Department | Die Abteilung, Die Abteilungen |
| Department (university) | Der Fachbereich, Die Fachbereiche |
| Department Head (school) | Der Fachleiter, Die Fachleiter, Die Fachleiterin, Die Fachleterinnen |
| Department Store | Das Kaufhaus, Die Kaufhäuser |
| Departure (flight) | Der Abflug, Die Abflüge |
| Departure (for a trip) | Die Abreise, Die Abreisen |
| Departure (vehicle, train) | Die Abfahrt, Die Abfahrten |
| Deposit (add to or insert) | Die Einlage, Die Einlagen |
| Deposit (money) | Die Einzahlung, Die Einzahlungen |
| Depot | Der Betriebshof, Die Betriebshöfe |

| English | German |
|---|---|
| Depression (economics, medical) | Die Depression, Die Depressionen |
| Depth | Die Tiefe, Die Tiefen |
| Description | Die Bezeichnung, Die Bezeichnungen |
| Desire | Die Lust, Die Lüste |
| Desk | Der Schreibtisch, Die Schreibtische |
| Destiny | Das Schicksal, Die Schicksale |
| Destruction (annihilation) | Die Vernichtung, Die Vernichtungen |
| Destruction (demolition) | Die Zerstörung, Die Zerstörungen |
| Detail | Das Detail, Die Details |
| Deterioration, Decay | Der Verfall |
| Determination | Der Will, Die Willen |
| Development | Die Entwicklung, Die Entwicklungen |
| Diamond | Der Diamant, Die Diamanten |
| Dictionary | Das Wörterbuch, Die Wörterbücher |
| Difference | Der Unterschied, Die Unterschiede |
| Difficulty | Die Schwierigkeit, Die Schwierigkeiten |
| Dignity | Die Würde |
| Dinner | Das Abendessen, Die Abendessen |
| Direction | Die Richtung, Die Richtungen |
| Dirt | Der Dreck |
| Dirt | Der Schmutz |
| Disbursement, Payout | Die Auszahlung, Die Auszahlungen |
| Disclaimer | Der Verzicht, Die Verzichte |
| Discontinuation | Die Abkündigung, Die Abkündigungen |
| Discount (rebate) | Der Rabatt, Die Rabatte |
| Disk, Hard Drive | Die Festplatte, Die Festplatten |
| Dispute | Der Streit, Die Streite |
| Distance | Der Abstand, Die Abstände |
| Distance | Die Distanz, Die Distanzen |
| Distance | Die Entfernung, Die Entfernungen |
| Distribution | Die Verteilung, Die Verteilungen |
| Diversity | Die Vielfalt |
| Divestment, Sale | Die Veräußerung, Die Veräußerungen |
| Dividend (finance) | Die Dividende, Die Dividenden |
| Dividend (fractions) | Der Dividend, Die Dividenden |
| Divorce | Die Scheidung, Die Scheidungen |
| Doctor, PhD | Der Doktor, Die Doktoren; Die Doktorin, Die Doktorinnen |
| Dog | Der Hund, Die Hunde |
| Dollar | Der Dollar, Die Dollars |
| Dolphin | Der Delphin, Die Delphine |
| Donkey | Der Esel, Die Esel |
| Door | Die Tür, Die Türen |

| English | German |
|---------|--------|
| Doorbell | Die Türklingel, Die Türklingeln |
| Doorhandle | Der Türgriff, Die Türgriffe |
| Doorknob | Der Türknauf, Die Türknäufe |
| Doorstep | Die Türschwelle, Die Türschwellen |
| Doorway | Die Türöffnung, Die Türöffnungen |
| Dorm (for students) | Das Studentenwohnheim, Die Studentenwohnheime |
| Double Room | Das Doppelzimmer, Die Doppelzimmer |
| Dough | Der Teig, Die Teige |
| Dragon | Der Drachen, Die Drachen |
| Drawer | Die Schublade, Die Schubladen |
| Drawing | Die Zeichnung, Die Zeichnungen |
| Dream | Der Traum, Die Träume |
| Dress | Das Kleid, Die Kleider |
| Drinking Straw | Der Trinkhalm, Die Trinkhalme |
| Driver | Der Fahrer, Die Fahrer |
| Driver seat | Der Fahrersitz, Die Fahrersitze |
| Driver's License | Der Führerschein, Die Führerscheine |
| Driveway | Die Einfahrt, Die Einfahrten |
| Drug (pharmacy) | Das Arzneimittel, Die Arzneimittel |
| Drug Store (not pharmacy) | Die Drogerie, Die Drogereien |
| Drum | Die Trommel, Die Trommeln |
| Duck | Die Ente, Die Enten |
| Dumdum | Der Dummkopf, Die Dummköpfe |
| Dust | Der Staub, Die Stäube |
| Dutch (language) | Das Niederländisch |
| Eagle | Der Adler, Die Adler |
| Ear | Das Ohr, Die Ohren |
| Earring | Der Ohrring, Die Ohrringe |
| Earth | Die Erde, Die Erden |
| Earthquake | Das Erdbeben, Die Erdbeben |
| Easing, Relaxation of | Die Lockerung, Die Lockerungen |
| East | Der Osten |
| Economics | Die Wirtschaftswissenhaften (used with singular verbs) |
| Economy | Die Wirtschaft, Die Wirtschaften |
| Edge | Die Kante, Die Kanten |
| Edge, Boundary | Der Rand, Die Ränder |
| Editor | Der Redakteur, Die Redakteure; Die Redakteurin, Die Redakteurinnen |
| Education, Training | Die Ausbildung, Die Ausbildungen |
| Eel | Der Aal, Die Aale |
| Effect (impact) | Die Wirkung, Die Wirkungen |
| Effect (ramification) | Die Auswirkung, Die Auswirkungen |

| English | German |
|---|---|
| Efficiency | Die Effizienz, Die Effizienzen |
| Effort | Der Aufwand, Die Aufwände |
| Effort | Die Anstrengung, Die Anstrengungen |
| Egg | Das Ei, Die Eier |
| Egg White | Das Eiweiß (example: *drei Eiweiß*) |
| Egg Yolk | Das Eigelb (example: *drei Eigelb*) |
| Eggplant | Die Aubergine, Die Auberginen |
| Elbow | Der Ellbogen, Die Ellenbogen |
| Election | Die Wahl, Die Wahlen |
| Election Campaign | Der Wahlkampf, Die Wahlkämpfe |
| Electric Stove | Der Elektroherd, Die Elektroherde |
| Electrician | Der Elektriker, Die Elektriker; Die Elektrikerin, Die Elektrikerinnen |
| Electron | Das Elektron, Die Elektronen |
| Electronics Store | Der Elektronikladen, Die Elektronikladen |
| Elephant | Der Elefant, Die Elefanten |
| Elevation | Die Erhebung, Die Erhebungen |
| Elevator | Der Aufzug, Die Aufzüge |
| Email | Die E-Mail, Die E-Mails |
| Embassy | Die Botschaft, Die Botschaften |
| Emergency | Der Notfall, Die Notfälle |
| Emergency Brake | Die Notbremse, Die Notbremsen |
| Emotion | Das Gefühl, Die Gefühle |
| Emphasis | Die Betonung, Die Betonungen |
| Empire | Das Imperium, Die Imperien |
| Employee, Salaried | Der Angestellte, Die Angestellten |
| Employee, Wage Earner | Der Arbeitnehmer, Die Arbeitnehmer; Die Arbeitnehmerin, Die Arbeitnehmerinnen |
| Employer | Der Arbeitgeber, Die Arbeitgeber; Die Arbeitgeberin, Die Arbeitgeberinnen |
| Employment | Die Beschäftigung, Die Beschäftigungen |
| Employment Contract | Der Arbeitsvertrag, Die Arbeitsverträge |
| End | Das Ende, Die Enden |
| End Table | Der Beistelltisch, Die Beistelltische |
| Engagement | Die Verlobung, Die Verlobung |
| Engagement Ring | Der Verlobungring, Die Verlobungringe |
| Engine | Der Motor, Die Motoren |
| English (language) | Das Englisch |
| Enjoyment | Das Vergnügen, Die Vergnügen |
| Enthusiasm | Die Begeisterung, Die Begeisterungen |
| Entry (into a place) | Der Einzug, Die Einzüge |
| Equal Opportunity | Die Chancengleichheit, Die Chancengleichheiten |
| Equal Right | Die Gleichberechtigung, Die Gleichberechtigungen |

| English | German |
|---|---|
| Equipment | Die Ausrüstung, Die Ausrüstungen |
| Error | Der Irrtum, Die Irrtümer |
| Essay | Der Aufsatz, Die Aufsätze |
| Estate, Inheritance | Der Nachlass, Die Nachlässe |
| Estate, Property | Das Anwesen, Die Anwesen |
| Estonian (language) | Das Estnisch |
| Etching | Die Radierung, Die Radierungen |
| Eternity | Die Ewigkeit, Die Ewigkeiten |
| Eucharist | Die Eucharistie |
| Euro | Der Euro, Die Euros |
| Evening | Der Abend, Die Abende |
| Event | Das Ereignis, Die Ereignisse |
| Everyday Life | Der Alltag |
| Exam | Das Exam, Die Examen |
| Example | Das Beispiel, Die Beispiele |
| Exchange (as in exchange student) | Der Austausch, Die Austausche |
| Exemption | Die Ausnahme, Die Ausnahmen |
| Existence | Die Existenz, Die Existenzen |
| Existentialism | Der Existenzialismus |
| Expectation | Die Erwartung, Die Erwartungen |
| Experience | Die Erfahrung, Die Erfahrungen |
| Experience | Das Erlebnis, Die Erlebnisse |
| Explanation, Declaration | Die Erklärung, Die Erklärungen |
| Explosive Substance | Der Sprengstoff, Die Sprengstoffe |
| Expression | Der Ausdruck, Die Ausdrücke |
| Expressionism | Der Expressionismus |
| Expressionist | Der Expressionist, Die Expressionisten; Die Expressionistin, Die Expressionistinnen |
| Extension Cord | Das Verlängerungskabel, Die Verlängerungskabel |
| Extent | Das Ausmaß, Die Ausmaße |
| Exterior, Outside | Die Außenseite, Die Außenseiten |
| Eye | Das Auge, Die Augen |
| Eye Shadow | Der Lidschatten, Die Lidschatten |
| Eyebrow | Die Augenbraue, Die Augenbrauen |
| Eyeglass Store | Das Optikergeschäft, Die Optikergeschäfte |
| Eyeglasses | Die Brille, Die Brillen |
| Eyelash | Die Wimper, Die Wimpern |
| Fabric | Der Stoff, Die Stoffe |
| Face | Das Gesicht, Die Gesichter |
| Facility (furnishings) | Die Einrichtung, Die Einrichtungen |
| Facility (park and castle together) | Die Anlage, Die Anlagen |
| Fact | Die Tatsache, Die Tatsachen |

| English | German |
|---|---|
| Fact Check | Der Faktencheck, Die Faktenchecks |
| Failure | Der Misserfolg, Die Misserfolge |
| Fairness, Righteousness | Die Gerechtigkeit |
| Fairy Tale | Das Märchen, Die Märchen |
| Fall, Collapse | Der Untergang, Die Untergänge |
| Family | Die Familie, Die Familien |
| Fan (sports) | Der Fan, Die Fans |
| Farewell | Der Abschied, Die Abschiede |
| Farewell, Sendoff | Die Verabschiedung, Die Verabschiedungen |
| Farm | Der Bauernhof, Die Bauernhöfe |
| Farmer | Der Bauer, Die Bauern; Die Bäuerin, Die Bäuerinnen |
| Fast (fasting time) | Die Fastenzeit, Die Fastenzeiten |
| Fat (for cooking) | Das Fett, Die Fette |
| Father | Der Vater, Die Väter |
| Father-in-law | Der Schwiegervater, Die Schwiegerväter |
| Fatigue | Die Müdigkeit |
| Favorite Food | Das Lieblingsessen, Die Lieblingsspeisen |
| Fear | Die Angst, Die Ängste |
| Feather | Die Feder, Die Federn |
| Feature | Das Merkmal, Die Merkmale |
| February | Der Februar |
| Fee | Die Gebühr, Die Gebühren |
| Feedback | Die Rückmeldung, Die Rückmeldungen |
| Feedback | Das Feedback, Die Feedbacks |
| Feedback (sound, guitar) | Die Rückkoppelung, Die Rückkoppelungen |
| Feeling | Das Gefühl, Die Gefühle |
| Ferry | Die Färhe, Die Fähren (can add a *Schiff* or *Boot* suffix) |
| Fertilizer | Der Dünger, Die Dünger |
| Festival | Das Fest, Die Feste |
| Fever | Das Fieber, Die Fieber |
| Field | Das Feld, Die Felder |
| Fife, Whistle | Die Pfeife, Die Pfeifen |
| Figure (in a play, physical traits) | Die Figur, Die Figuren |
| Film Camera | Die Filmkamera, Die Filmkameras |
| Final Exam (academic high school) | Das Abitur |
| Finger | Der Finger, Die Finger |
| Finnish (language) | Das Finnisch |
| Fire | Das Feuer, Die Feuer |
| Fireman | Der Feuerwehrmann, Die Feuerwehrmänner |
| Fireplace | Der Kamin, Die Kamine |

| English | German |
|---------|--------|
| Firewoman | Die Feuerwehrfrau, Die Feuerfehrfrauen |
| Fish | Der Fisch, Die Fische |
| Fist | Die Faust, Die Fäuste |
| Flavor | Der Geschmack, Die Geschmäcke |
| Flea Market | Der Flohmarkt, Die Flohmärkte |
| Fleet | Die Flotte, Die Flotten |
| Flight | Der Flug, Die Flüge |
| Flight Number | Die Flugnummer, Die Flugnummern |
| Flock | Der Schwarm, Die Schwärme |
| Floor | Der Boden, Die Böden |
| Floor, Story (building) | Der Stock, Die Stock |
| Flour | Das Mehl, Die Mehle |
| Flower | Die Blume, Die Blumen |
| Flower Shop | Der Blumenladen, Die Blumenladen |
| Flute | Die Flöte, Die Flöten |
| Focus, Main Point | Der Schwerpunkt, Die Schwerpunkte |
| Fog | Der Nebel, Die Nebel |
| Folder (file) | Der Ordner, Die Ordner |
| Folk, Public | Das Volk, Die Völker |
| Food | Die Speise, Die Speisen |
| Food | Das Essen |
| Fool | Der Narr, Die Narren; Die Närrin, Die Närrinnen |
| Foolishness | Die Dummheit |
| Foot | Der Fuß, Die Füße |
| Forces | Die Kraft, Die Kräfte |
| Forehead | Die Stirn, Die Stirnen |
| Foreign Language | Die Fremdsprache, Die Fremdsprachen |
| Forest | Der Forst, Die Forste |
| Forest Fire | Der Waldbrand, Die Waldbrände |
| Fork | Die Gabel, Die Gabeln |
| Form | Die Form, Die Formen |
| Form (paper) | Das Formular, Die Formulare |
| Fortress, Fortification | Die Festung, Die Festungen |
| Forum | Das Forum, Die Foren |
| Foundation | Die Gründung, Die Gründungen |
| Foyer | Die Wandelhalle, Die Wandelhallen |
| Frame | Der Rahmen, Die Rahmen |
| Fraud | Der Betrug, Die Betrüger |
| Freak | Der Freak, Die Freaks |
| Freedom | Die Freiheit |
| French (language) | Das Französisch |
| French Horn | Das Waldhorn, Die Waldhörner |
| Friction | Die Reibung, Die Reibungen |

| English | German |
|---|---|
| Friday | Der Freitag, Die Freitage |
| Friend | Der Freund, Die Freunde |
| Friendship | Die Freundschaft, Die Freundschaften |
| Frisian (language) | Das Friesisch |
| Front | Die Front, Die Fronten |
| Fruit | Die Frucht, Die Früchte |
| Fruit | Das Frucht, Die Früchte |
| Fruit (the plant seed) | Das Obst |
| Fryer | Die Fritteuse, Die Fritteusen |
| Full-time Work | Die Vollzeitarbeit |
| Fun | Der Spaß, Die Späße |
| Function | Die Funktion, Die Funktionen |
| Funeral | Die Beerdigung, Die Beerdigung |
| Furnace | Der Heizofen, Die Heizöfen |
| Furniture | Die Möbel |
| Future | Die Zukunft |
| Futures (financial) | Das Termingeschäft, Die Termingeschäfte |
| Gaelic (language) | Das Gälisch |
| Game | Das Spiel, Die Spiele |
| Gap, Chasm, Cleft (between things, such as rich and poor) | Die Kluft, Die Klüfte |
| Gap, Void (missing piece, such as in knowledge) | Die Lücke, Die Lücken |
| Garage | Die Garagen, Die Garagen |
| Garbage | Der Abfall, Die Abfälle |
| Garden | Der Garten, Die Gärten |
| Garlic | Der Knoblauch |
| Garlic Press | Die Knoblauchpresse, Die Knoblauchpressen |
| Gas Stove | Der Gasherd, Die Gasherde |
| Gas, Petrol | Das Benzin, Die Benzine |
| Gate | Das Tor, Die Tore |
| Gear (car, bike) | Der Gang, Die Gänge |
| Gelding | Der Wallach, Die Wallache |
| Gemini | Der Zwilling, Die Zwillinge |
| Gender (language) | Das Genus, Die Genera |
| Gender (sex) | Das Geschlecht, Die Geschlechter |
| Gene | Das Gen, Die Gene |
| Generosity | Die Großzügigkeit, Die Großzügigkeiten |
| Gentleman, Lord | Der Herr, Die Herren |
| German (language) | Das Deutsch |
| German State | Der Bundesstaat, Die Bundesländer |
| Ghost | Der Geist, Die Geister |
| Gift | Das Geschenk, Die Geschenke |
| Gin | Der Gin, Die Gins |

| English | German |
|---------|--------|
| Ginger | Die Ingwerwurzel, Die Ingwerwurzeln |
| Giraffe | Die Giraffe, Die Giraffen |
| Girl | Das Mädchen, Die Mädchen |
| Girlfriend | Die Freundin, Die Freundinnen |
| Giver | Der Geber, Die Geber; Die Geberin, Die Geberinnen |
| Glamor | Der Glamour |
| Glass | Das Glas, Die Gläser |
| Global Economy | Die Weltwirtschaft, Die Weltwirtschaften |
| Globalization | Der Globalizierung |
| Glove | Der Hanschuh, Die Handschuhe |
| Gnat | Die Mücke, Die Mücken |
| Goal (as in scoring a goal) | Das Tor, Die Tore |
| Goal (as in working toward a goal) | Das Ziel, Die Ziele |
| Goal Post | Der Pfosten, Die Pfosten |
| Goalie | Der Torwart, Die Torwarte; Die Torwartin, Die Torwartinnen |
| Goat | Die Ziege, Die Ziegen |
| Goat, Billy | Der Ziegenbock, Die Ziegenböcke |
| God | Der Gott, Die Götter |
| Gold | Das Gold |
| Gold Medal | Die Goldmedaille, Die Goldmedaillen |
| Good-for-Nothing (as in the memoirs of von Eichendorff) | Der Taugenichts, Die Taugenichtse |
| Goose | Die Gans, Die Gänse |
| Gooseberry | Die Stachelbeere, Die Stachelbeeren |
| Gorilla | Der Gorilla, Die Gorillas |
| Government | Die Regierung, Die Regierungen |
| Grace | Die Gnade, Die Gnaden |
| Grade (military, weather, math) | Der Grad, Die Grade |
| Grandfather | Der Großvater, Die Großväter |
| Grandmother | Die Großmutter, Die Großmütter |
| Grape | Die Traube, Die Trauben |
| Grape Juice | Der Traubensaft, Die Traubensäfte |
| Grass | Das Gras, Die Gräser |
| Great White Shark | Der Weiße Hai, Die weißen Haie |
| Greek (language) | Das Griechisch |
| Grenade | Die Granate, Die Granaten |
| Groceries | Die Lebensmittel |
| Group | Die Gruppe, Die Gruppen |
| Growth | Das Wachstum |

| English | German |
|---------|--------|
| Guard | Der Wächter, Die Wächter; Die Wächterin, Die Wächterinnen |
| Guardian | Der Hüter, Die Hüter; Die Hüterin, Die Hüterinnen |
| Guest | Der Gast, Die Gäste |
| Guidance | Die Führung, Die Führungen |
| Guideline | Die Richtlinie, Die Richtlinien |
| Guinea Pig | Das Meerschweinchen, Die Meerschweinchen |
| Guitar | Die Gitarre, Die Gitarren |
| Gulf | Der Golf, Die Gölfe |
| Gun | Die Waffe, Die Waffen |
| Gust | Der Windstoß, Die Windstöße |
| Guy | Der Kerl, Die Kerle |
| Gym (commercial) | Das Fitnessstudio, Die Fitnessstudios |
| Gym Shoe | Der Turnschuh, Die Turnschuhe (usually plural) |
| Gym, School | Die Turnhall, Die Turnhallen |
| Hail | Der Hagel |
| Hair | Das Haar, Die Haare |
| Half | Die Hälfte, Die Hälften |
| Halftime | Die Halbzeit, Die Halbzeite |
| Halibut | Der Heilbutt |
| Hall | Die Halle, Die Hallen |
| Hallway | Der Flur, Die Flure |
| Hamster | Der Hamster, Die Hamster |
| Hand | Die Hand, Die Hände |
| Handbag | Die Handtasche, Die Handtaschen |
| Handkerchief | Das Taschentuch, Die Taschentücher |
| Handover | Die Übergabe, Die Übergaben |
| Hardship, Misery | Das Elend |
| Hardware Store | Das Haushaltswarengeschäft, Die Haushaltswarengeschäfte |
| Hardware, Part, Component (computer) | Das Computerteil, Die Computerteile |
| Harmony | Der Einklang, Die Einklänge |
| Hat | Der Hut, Die Hüte |
| Hate Speech | Die Hassrede |
| Hay | Das Heu |
| Hazelnut | Die Haselnuss, Die Haselnüsse |
| Head | Der Kopf, Die Köpfe |
| Header (soccer) | Der Kopfball, Die Kopfbälle |
| Headhunter | Der Kopfjäger, Die Kopfjäger; Die Kopfjägerin, Die Kopfjägerinnen |
| Headlight | Der Scheinwerfer, Die Scheinwerfer |
| Health | Die Gesundheit |

| English | German |
|---------|--------|
| Hearing | Das Gehör, Die Gehöre |
| Heart | Das Herz, Die Herzen |
| Heat | Die Hitze |
| Hebrew (language) | Das Hebräisch |
| Height | Die Höhe, Die Höhen |
| Height Increase | Die Höhenzunahme, Die Höhenzunahmen |
| Helicopter | Der Hubschrauber, Die Hubschrauber |
| Hell | Die Hölle, Die Höllen |
| Help | Die Hilfe, Die Helfin |
| Herd | Die Herde, Die Herden |
| Herdsman | Der Hirte, Die Hirten; Die Hirterin, Die Hirterinnen |
| Herring | Der Hering |
| Herringbone Pattern | Der Fischgrätmuster, Die Fischgrätmuster |
| Hike | Das Wandern, Die Wanderungen |
| Hill | Der Hügel, Die Hügel |
| Hindi (language) | Das Hindi |
| Hindrance | Das Hindernis, Die Hindernisse |
| Hinduism | Der Hinduismus |
| Hint | Der Hinweis, Die Hinweise |
| History | Die Geschichte, Die Geschichten |
| Hole | Das Loch, Die Löcher |
| Holiday | Der Feiertag, Die Feiertagen |
| Home | Die Heimat, Die Heime |
| Home | Das Zuhause |
| Home, Asylum | Das Heim, Die Heime |
| Homework | Die Hausaufgaben |
| Honey | Der Honig, Die Honige |
| Honeymoon | Die Flitterwochen (plural used as singular) |
| Hope | Die Hoffnung, Die Hoffnungen |
| Hornet | Die Hornisse, Die Hornissen |
| Horror, Fright | Der Schrecken, Die Schrecken |
| Horse | Das Pferd, Die Pferde |
| Hospital | Das Krankenhaus, Die Krankenhäuser |
| Hostel | Die Jugendherberge, Die Jugendherbergen |
| Hotel | Das Hotel, Die Hotels |
| Hour | Die Stunde, Die Stunden |
| House | Das Haus, Die Häuser |
| House (timbered) | Das Fachwerkhaus, Die Fachwerkhäuser |
| House of Representatives | Das Abgeordnetenhaus |
| Household | Der Haushalt, Die Haushalte |
| Human | Der Mensch, Die Menschen |
| Humanity | Die Menschlichkeit, Die Menschlichkeiten |
| Hungarian (language) | Das Ungarisch |

| English | German |
|---|---|
| Husband | Der Ehemann, Die Ehemänner |
| Husband | Der Mann, Die Männer |
| Ice | Das Eis |
| Ice Skate | Der Schlittschuh, Die Schlittschuhe |
| Icelandic (language) | Das Isländisch |
| Icing, Glazing | Die Glasur, Die Glasuren |
| ID Card | Der Ausweis, Die Ausweise |
| Idea | Die Idee, Die Ideen |
| Ideology | Die Ideologie, Die Ideologien |
| Idiot | Der Idiot, Die Idioten; Die Idiotin, Die Idiotinnen |
| Image | Das Bild, Die Bilder |
| Imagination | Die Vorstellungskraft, Die Vorstellungskräfte |
| Impact | Die Auswirkung, Die Auswirkungenen |
| Importance | Die Wichtigkeit |
| Impression | Der Eindruck, Die Eindrücke |
| Impressionism | Der Impressionismus |
| Impressionist | Der Impressionist, Die Impressionisten; Die Impressionistin, Die Impressionistinnen |
| Inability | Die Unfähigkeit, Die Unfähigkeiten |
| Inauguration (of something new) | Die Einweihung, Die Einweihungen |
| Inauguration (Office, Presidential) | Die Amtseinführung, Die Amtseinführungen |
| Income, Earnings | Das Einkommen, Die Einkommen |
| Increase (add to) | Die Zunahme, Die Zunahmen (from *zunehmen*) |
| Increase (climb) | Die Steigerung, Die Steigerungen (from *steigen*) |
| Independence, 4th of July | Die Unabhängigkeit |
| Independence, Self-Reliance | Die Selbständigkeit |
| Index Finger | Der Zeigefinger, Die Zeigefinger |
| Indication | Die Angabe, Die Angaben |
| Individual | Der Einzelner, Die Einzelne; Die Einzelne, Die Einzelne |
| Industry | Die Industrie, Die Industrien |
| Infection | Die Infektion, Die Infektionen |
| Infection, Contagion | Die Ansteckung, Die Ansteckungen |
| Infinity | Die Unendlichkeit, Die Unendlichkeiten |
| Information | Die Auskunft, Die Auskünfte |
| Information, Specification, Indication | Die Angabe, Die Angaben |
| Ingredient | Die Zutat, Die Zutaten |
| Insect | Das Insekt, Die Insekten |
| Insight | Der Einblick, Die Einblicke |
| Inspector | Der Inspektor, Die Inspektoren; Die Inspektorin, Die Inspektorinnen |

| English | German |
|---------|--------|
| Instance, Case, Event | Der Fall, Die Fälle |
| Instruction, Information | Die Unterrichtung, Die Unterrichtungen |
| Insult, Affront | Die Beleidigung, Die Beleidigungen |
| Insurance | Die Versicherung, Die Versicherungen |
| Insurer | Der Versicherer, Die Versicherer |
| Integration, Inclusion | Die Eingliederung, Die Eingliederungen |
| Intention | Die Absicht, Die Absichten |
| Interest | Die Interesse, Die Interessen |
| Interest (on money) | Der Zins, Die Zinsen |
| Interference | Der Eingriff, Die Eingriffe |
| Internet | Das Internet |
| Interruption | Die Unterbrechung, Die Unterbrechungen |
| Intersection | Die Kreuzung, Die Kreuzungen |
| Interview | Das Vorstellungsgespräch, Die Vorstellungsgespräche |
| Inventory, Supply | Der Vorrat, Die Vorräte |
| Inversion | Die Umkehrung, Die Umkehrungen |
| Investment | Die Investition, Die Investitionen |
| Iran | Der Iran |
| Iraq | Der Irak |
| Island | Die Insel, Die Inseln |
| Italian (language) | Das Italienisch |
| Item, Object, Article | Der Gegenstand, Die Gegenstände |
| Ivory Coast | Die Elfenbeinküste |
| Jacket | Die Jacke, Die Jacken |
| Jam, Preserves, Fruit Spread | Die Konfitüre, Die Konfitüren |
| January | Der Januar |
| Japanese (language) | Das Japanisch |
| Jealousy | Die Eifersucht, Die Eifersüchte |
| Jeans | Die Jeans |
| Jelly | Das Gelee, Die Gelees |
| Jellyfish | Die Qualle, Die Quallen |
| Jersey (soccer) | Das Trikot, Die Trikots |
| Jewelry | Der Schmuck, Die Schmucken |
| Jewelry Store | Der Schmuckladen, Die Schmuckläden |
| Job | Der Job, Die Jobs |
| Job Application | Die Bewerbung, Die Bewerbungen |
| Job Site | Die Baustelle, Die Baustellen |
| Joke | Der Witz, Die Witze |
| Judge | Der Richter, Die Richter; Die Richterin, Die Richterinnen |
| Judgement | Das Urteil, Die Urteile |
| Juice | Der Saft, Die Säfte |
| July | Der Juli |

| English | German |
|---|---|
| June | Der Juni |
| Jungle | Der Dschungel, Die Dschungel |
| Kangaroo | Das Känguru, Die Kängurus |
| Ketchup | Der Ketchup, Die Ketchudps |
| Key | Der Schlüssel, Die Schlüssel |
| Keyboard | Die Tastatur, Die Tastaturen |
| Kinesiology | Die Kinesiology |
| King | Der König, Die Könige |
| Kitchen | Die Küche, Die Küchen |
| Kitchen Scale | Die Küchenwaage, Die Küchenwaagen |
| Kite | Der Drachen, Die Drachen |
| Kiwi | Die Kiwi, Die Kiwis |
| Knee | Das Knie, Die Knie |
| Knife | Das Messer, Die Messer |
| Knowledge | Das Wissen |
| Korean (language) | Das Koreanisch |
| Kurdish (language) | Das Kurdisch |
| Ladder | Die Leiter, Die Leitern |
| Ladle | Der Schöplöffel, Die Löffel |
| Ladle (food) | Die Schöpfkelle, Die Schöpfkellen |
| Ladle (metallurgy) | Die Gießpfanne, Die Gießpfannen |
| Lady | Die Dame, Die Damen |
| Lager, Beer | Das Export |
| Lake | Der See, Die Seen |
| Lamb | Das Lamm, Die Lämmer |
| Lamp | Die Lampe, Die Lampen |
| Lamppost, Streetlight | Die Laterne, Die Laternen |
| Land | Das Land, Die Ländereien |
| Language | Die Sprache, Die Sprachen |
| Lap | Der Schoß, Die Schöße |
| Laps, sport | Die Runden, Die Runden |
| Laptop | Der Laptop, Die Laptops |
| Latin (language) | Das Latein |
| Latvian (language) | Das Lettisch |
| Lava | Die Lava, Die Laven |
| Law | Das Gesetz, Die Gesetze |
| Lawn Mower | Der Rasenmäher, Die Rasenmäher |
| Lawsuit | Die Klage, Die Klagen |
| Lawyer | Der Anwalt, Die Anwälte; Die Anwältin, Die Anwältinnen |
| Layoff | Die Personalkürzung, Die Personalkürzung |
| Lead (metal) | Das Blei |
| Leader, Director | Der Leiter, Die Leiter; Die Leiterin, Die Leiterinnen |

| English | German |
| --- | --- |
| Leadership | Die Führung, Die Führungen |
| Leaf | Das Blatt, Die Blätter |
| Leather | Das Leder, Die Leder |
| Lebanon | Der Libanon |
| Lecture, Presentation | Der Vortrag, Die Vorträge |
| Lecture, University | Die Vorlesung, Die Vorlesungen |
| Leg | Das Bein, Die Beine |
| Lemon | Die Zitrone, Die Zitronen |
| Lending, Loan Activity | Die Kreditvergabe, Die Kreditvergaben |
| Length (math, determined by a ruler) | Die Länge, Die Längen |
| Leo | Der Löwe, Die Löwen |
| Letter | Der Brief, Die Briefe |
| Lettuce | Der Salat, Die Salate |
| Lettuce Head | Der Kopfsalat (also Der Salat), Die Kopfsalate |
| Lettuce, Romaine | Der Römersalat, Die Römersalate |
| Liberator | Der Befreier, Die Befreier; Die Befreierin, Die Befreierinnen |
| Libra | Die Waage, Die Waagen |
| Library | Die Bibliothek, Die Bibliotheken |
| License Plate | Das Kennzeichenschild, Die Kennzeichenschilder |
| License Plate | Das Nummernschild, Die Nummernschilder |
| Life | Das Leben, Die Leben |
| Lifeguard | Der Beidemeister, Die Beidemeistern; Die Beidemeisterin, Die Beidemeisterinnen |
| Lifeguard | Der Rettungsschwimmer, Die Rettungsschwimmer; Die Rettungsschwimmerin, Die Rettungsschwimmerinnen |
| Light | Das Licht, Die Lichter |
| Lightning | Der Blitz, Die Blitze |
| Limb (anatomy) | Das Glied, Die Glieder |
| Lime | Die Limone, Die Limonen |
| Line | Die Linie, Die Linien |
| Line (telephone) | Die Leitung, Die Leitungen |
| Lion | Der Löwe, Die Löwen; Die Löwin, Die Löwinnen |
| Lip | Die Lippe, Die Lippen |
| Lipstick | Der Lippenstift, Die Lippenstifte |
| List | Die Liste, Die Listen |
| Listener | Der Zuhörer, Die Zuhörer; Die Zuhörerin, Die Zuhörerinnen |
| Literature | Die Literatur, Die Literaturen |
| Lithuanian (language) | Das Litauisch |
| Livestock | Das Vieh |

| English | German |
| --- | --- |
| Living | Die Lebenden |
| Load, Burden | Die Last, Die Lasten |
| Lobby (hotel) | Die Lobby, Die Lobbys |
| Lobster | Der Hummer, Die Hummer |
| Locals | Die Einheimischen |
| Location (fixed) | Der Standort, Die Standorte |
| Location, Position | Die Lage, Die Lagen |
| Lord | Der Herr, Die Herren |
| Loss | Der Verlust, Die Verluste |
| Lot (situation, the what's-going-on) | Das Los, Die Lose |
| Love | Die Liebe, Die Liebe |
| Lug Nuts | Die Radmutter, Die Radmuttern |
| Luggage | Das Gepäck |
| Lunch | Das Mittagessen, Die Mittagessen |
| Lunch Break | Die Mittagspause, Die Mittagspausen |
| Machine | Die Maschine, Die Maschinen |
| Madam | Die Dame, Die Damen |
| Magazine | Die Zeitschrift, Die Zeitschriften |
| Magazine Cover | Die Titelseite |
| Magnate | Der Magnat, Die Magnaten; Die Magnatin, Die Magnatinnen |
| Mail | Die Post |
| Mailbox | Der Briefkasten, Die Briefkästen |
| Mailbox | Das Postfach, Die Postfächer |
| Main, Head, Primary (as a prefix) | Das Haupt, Die Häupter |
| Mainstream | Die Hauptrichtung, Die Hauptrichtungen |
| Maintenance (preventive) | Die Wartung, Die Wartungen |
| Major (college) | Das Hauptfach, Die Hauptfächer |
| Majority | Die Mehrheit, Die Mehrheiten |
| Makeup Foundation | Das Make-up |
| Makeup Items | Die Schminke (example: *Ich schminke mich*) |
| Mall | Das Einkaufszentrum, Die Einkaufszentren |
| Man | Der Mann, Die Männer |
| Manager, Business Director | Der Geschäftsführer, Die Geschäftsführer; Die Geschäftsführerin, Die Geschäftsführerinnen |
| Mandarin (language) | Das Mandarin |
| Mango | Die Mango, Die Mangos |
| Manor, Country Estate | Der Landsitz, Die Landsitze |
| Manor, Estate | Das Landgut, Die Landgüter |
| Manufacturer | Der Hersteller, Die Hersteller |
| Marathon | Der Marathon, Die Marathons |
| March | Der März |

| English | German |
|---|---|
| Mare | Die Stute, Die Stuten |
| Market | Der Markt, Die Märkte |
| Markup, Price Increase | Der Aufschlag, Die Aufschläge |
| Marmalade | Die Marmelade, Die Marmeladen |
| Marriage | Die Ehe, Die Ehen |
| Married Couple | Das Ehepaar, Die Ehepaare |
| Mascara | Die Wimperntusche, Die Wimperntuschen |
| Mass, Holy Mass | Die Messe, Die Heilige Messe |
| Master | Der Meister, Die Meister |
| Math, Mathematics | Die Mathematik |
| Matter, Substance | Die Substanz, Die Substanzen |
| Maximum | Das Maximum, Die Maxima |
| May | Der Mai |
| Meadow | Die Wiese, Die Wiesen |
| Meaning | Die Bedeutung, Die Bedeutungen |
| Measles | Die Masern |
| Measure (of action) | Die Maßnahme, Die Maßnahmen |
| Measuring Cup | Der Messbecher, Die Messbecher |
| Measuring Spoon | Der Messlöffel, Die Messlöffeln |
| Meat, Flesh | Das Fleisch |
| Medal | Die Medaille, Die Medaillen |
| Media | Die Medien |
| Medication, Drug, Medicine | Das Medikament, Die Medikamenten |
| Meeting | Das Treffe, Die Treffen |
| Meeting (sitting down) | Die Sitzung, Die Sitzungen |
| Member | Das Mitglied, Die Mitglieder |
| Member of a Family | Der Angehörige, Die Angehörigen |
| Membership | Die Mitgliedschaft, Die Mitgliedschaften |
| Memory | Die Erinnerung, Die Erinnerungen |
| Memory, not electronic | Das Gedächtnis, Die Gedächtnisse |
| Mess, Untidiness, Clutter | Die Unordentlichkeit |
| Message | Die Nachricht, Die Nachrichten |
| Message, Report | Die Meldung, Die Meldungen |
| Metal | Das Metall, Die Metalle |
| Metaphor | Die Metapher, Die Metaphern |
| Method | Die Methode, Die Methoden |
| Metro Area | Der Großraum, Die Großräume |
| Microphone | Das Mikrofon, Die Mikrofone |
| Middle | Die Mitte, Die Middles |
| Midfield | Das Mittelfeld, Die Mittelfelder |
| Midnight | Die Mitternacht |
| Might, Power | Die Macht, Die Mächte |
| Milk | Die Milch |

| English | German |
|---|---|
| Millions | Die Millionen |
| Mind, Sense | Der Sinn, Die Sinne |
| Minimalism | Der Minimalismus |
| Minimalist | Der Minimalist, Die Minimalisten; Die Minimalistin, Die Minimalistinnen |
| Minor (college) | Das Nebenfach, Die Nebenfächer |
| Minority | Die Minderheit, Die Minderheiten |
| Minute | Der Minut, Die Minuten |
| Mirror | Der Spiegel, Die Spiegel |
| Mist, Haze | Der Dunst, Die Dünste |
| Mistake | Der Fehler, Die Fehler |
| Mixer | Der Handmixer, Die Handmixer |
| Model (person or thing, such as a fashion model or airplane model) | Das Modell, Die Modelle |
| Molecule | Das Molekül, Die Moleküle |
| Mom | Die Mama, Die Mamas |
| Moment | Der Moment, Die Momente |
| Monday | Der Montag, Die Montage |
| Money | Das Geld, Die Gelder |
| Mongolia | Die Mongolei |
| Monkey | Die Affe, Die Affen, Die Äffin, Die Äffinnen |
| Month | Der Monat, Die Monate |
| Moon | Der Mond, Die Monde |
| Moonlight (from the moon) | Das Mondlicht |
| Moonlighting | Die Schwarzarbeit, Die Schwarzarbeiten |
| Morning | Der Morgen, Die Morgen |
| Mosquito | Der Moskito, Die Moskitos (also Die Stechmücke) |
| Mosquito | Die Stechmücke, Die Stechmücken (also Der Moskito) |
| Mother | Die Mutter, Die Mütter |
| Mother-in-law | Die Schwiegermutter, Die Schwiegermütter |
| Mountain | Der Berg, Die Berge |
| Mouse | Der Maus, Die Mäuse |
| Mouth | Der Mund, Die Münder |
| Movement | Die Bewegung, Die Bewegungen |
| Movie | Der Film, Die Filme |
| Mud | Der Schlamm |
| Mule | Das Maultier, Die Maultiere |
| Municipality | Die Gemeinde, Die Gemeinden |
| Museum | Das Museum, Die Museen |
| Mushroom (cooking) | Der Champignon, Die Champignons |
| Mushroom (fungus) | Der Pilz, Die Pilze |
| Music | Die Musik, Die Musiken |

| English | German |
|---|---|
| Muslim | Der Muslim, Die Muslime |
| Mussel | Die Miessmuschel, Die Miessmuscheln |
| Mustard | Der Senf, Die Senfe |
| Nail Polish | Der Nagellack, Die Nagellacke |
| Name | Der Name, Die Namen |
| Name, First | Der Vorname, Die Vornamen |
| Nap, Snooze | Das Nickerchen, Die Nickerchen |
| Narcotic | Das Betäubungsmittel, Die Betäubungsmittel |
| Narrator | Der Erzähler, Die Erzähler; Die Erzählerin, Die Erzählerinnen |
| Nationalist | Der Nationalist, Die Nationalisten |
| Native | Der Ureinwohner, Die Ureinwohner; Die Ureinwohnerin, Die Ureinwohnerinnen |
| Nature | Die Natur, Die Naturen |
| Navel | Der Bauchnabel, Die Bauchnabel |
| Navy | Die Marine, Die Marinen |
| Neck | Der Hals, Die Hälse |
| Necklace | Die Halskette, Die Halsketten |
| Necktie | Die Krawatte, Die Krawatten |
| Need | Das Bedürfnis, Die Bedürfnisse |
| Needle | Die Nadel, Die Nadeln |
| Neglect | Die Vernachlässigung, Die Vernachlässigungen |
| Negligence | Die Nachlässigkeit, Die Nachlässigkeiten |
| Negotiation | Die Verhandlung, Die Verhandlungen |
| Neighbor | Der Nachbar, Die Nachbarn |
| Neighborhood | Die Nachbarschaft, Die Nachbarschaften |
| Neon | Das Neon |
| Nephew | Der Neffe, Die Neffen |
| Nest | Das Nest, Die Nester |
| Netherlands | Die Niederlande |
| Neurotic | Die Neurose, Die Neurosen |
| Neutron | Das Neutron, Die Neutronen |
| News | Die Nachrichten |
| News Portal | Das Nachrichtenportal, Die Nachrichtenportale |
| Newspaper | Die Zeitung, Die Zeitungen |
| Niece | Die Nichte, Die Nichten |
| Night | Die Nacht, Die Nächte |
| Night Shift | Die Nachtschicht, Die Nachtschicht |
| Nightmares | Der Albtraum, Die Albträume |
| Nihilism | Der Nihilismus |
| Nihilist | Der Nihilist, Die Nihilisten; Die Nihilistin, Die Nihilistinnen |
| Nobility | Der Adel |
| Noise | Der Lärm |

133

| English | German |
|---|---|
| Noise | Das Geräusch, Die Geräusche |
| Noodle | Die Nudel, Die Nudeln |
| Noon | Der Mittag, Die Mittage |
| Noon Hour | Die Mittagstunde, Die Mittagstunden |
| North | Der Norden |
| Norwegian (language) | Das Norwegisch |
| Nose | Die Nase, Die Nasen |
| Note | Die Notiz, Die Notizen |
| Note (school grade, banknote, musical) | Die Note, Die Noten |
| Nothing | Das Nichts |
| Notion, Idea, Concept | Der Begriff, Die Begriffe |
| Noun | Das Substantiv, Die Substantive |
| Novel | Der Roman, Die Romane |
| November | Der November |
| Nuclear Power (electricity) | Die Kernkraft, Die Kernkräfte |
| Nuclear Power (military) | Die Atomkraft |
| Nuclear Power Plant | Das Kernkraftwerk, Die Kernkraftwerke |
| Number | Die Nummer, Die Nummern |
| Number | Die Zahl, Die Zählen |
| Numeral, Cypher | Die Ziffer, Die Ziffern |
| Nurse (female) | Die Krankenschwester, Die Krankenschwestern |
| Nurse, male | Der Krankenpfleger, Die Krankenpflegerin |
| Nursing Home | Das Pflegeheim, Die Pflegeheime |
| Nut | Die Nuss, Die Nüsse |
| Nutcracker | Der Nussknacker, Die Nussknacker |
| Object (grammar, astronomy) | Das Objekt, Die Objekte |
| Obligation, Duty | Die Pflicht, Die Pflichten |
| Oboe | Die Oboe, Die Oboen |
| Obstacle | Das Hindernis, Die Hindernisse |
| Occupation | Der Beruf, Die Berufe |
| October | Der Oktober |
| Octopus | Der Oktopus, Die Oktopusse |
| Offer | Das Angebot, Die Angebote |
| Office | Das Büro, Die Büros |
| Officer | Der Offizier, Die Offiziere; Die Offizierin, Die Offizierinnen |
| Offsides (sports) | Das Abseits, Die Abseits |
| Oil | Das Öl, Die Öle |
| Oil Tanker | Der Öltanker, Die Öltanker |
| Oligarchy | Die Oligarchie, Die Oligarchien |
| Olive Oil | Das Olivenöl, Die Olivenöle |
| Olympic Games | Die Olympiade, Die Olympiaden |

| English | German |
|---------|--------|
| Oman | Der Oman |
| One | Der Eine, Die Einen |
| One-way Street | Die Einbahnstraße, Die Einbahnstraßen |
| Onion | Der Zwiebel, Die Zwiebeln |
| Operation (medical) | Die Operation, Die Operationen |
| Operator | Der Betreiber, Die Betreiber; Die Betreiberin, Die Betreiberinnen |
| Opinion | Die Meinung, Die Meinungen |
| Opponent | Der Gegner, Die Gegner; Die Gegnerin, Die Gegnerinnen |
| Opportunity | Die Gelegenheit, Die Gelegenheiten |
| Opposite | Das Gegenteil, Die Gegenteile |
| Optimism | Der Optimismus |
| Optimist | Der Optimist, Die Optimisten; Die Optimistin, Die Optimistinnen |
| Orange (color) | Das Orange, Die Orange |
| Orange (fruit) | Die Apfelsine, Die Apfelsinen |
| Orange Juice | Der Orangensaft, Die Orangensafte |
| Order (buying or reserving) | Die Bestellung, Die Bestellungen |
| Order, Tidiness | Die Ordnung |
| Orderliness | Die Ordentlichkeit |
| Organ, Music | Die Orgel, Die Orgeln |
| Organization, Enterprise | Der Betrieb, Die Betriebe |
| Origin | Der Ursprung, Die Ursprünge |
| Others | Die Anderen, Die Anderen |
| Outbreak | Der Ausbruch, Die Ausbrüche |
| Outcome, Result | Das Ergebnis, Die Ergebnisse |
| Oven | Der Backofen, Die Backöfen |
| Overcoming | Die Überwindung, Die Überwindungen |
| Oversight, Mistake | Das Versehen, Die Versehen |
| Overtime | Die Überstunde, Die Überstunden |
| Owner | Das Innere |
| Oyster | Die Auster, Die Austern |
| Pacific | Der Pazifik |
| Pacifist | Der Pazifist, Die Pazifisten; Die Pazifistin, Die Pazifistinnen |
| Pact | Das Abkommen, Die Abkommen |
| Page | Die Seite, Die Seiten |
| Pain (bodily) | Der Schmerz, Die Schmerzen |
| Paint | Die Farbe, Die Farben |
| Painting | Das Gemälde, Die Gemälde |
| Pair | Das Paar, Die Paare |
| Palm | Die Handfläche, Die Handflächen |
| Pant | Die Hose, Die Hosen |

| English | German |
|---------|--------|
| Panties | Das Höschen, Die Höschen |
| Pantsuit | Der Hosenanzug, Die Hosenanzüge |
| Paper | Das Papier, Die Papiere |
| Paper Cash, Bill | Der Geldschein, Die Geldscheine |
| Paprika | Die Paprika |
| Parachute | Der Fallschirm, Die Falllschirme |
| Parachutist | Der Fallschirmspringer, Die Fallschirmspringer; Die Fallschirmspringerin, Die Fallschirmspringerinnen |
| Paradise | Das Paradies, Die Paradiese |
| Parent | Das Eltern, Die Eltern |
| Parental Allowance | Das Elterngeld, Die Elterngelder |
| Parenthood | Die Elternschaft |
| Paring Knife | Das Gemüssemesser, Die Gemüssemesser |
| Park | Der Park, Die Parks |
| Parliament (Germany) | Der Bundestag |
| Parliament, People's Representation | Die Volksvertretung, Die Volksvertretungen |
| Parrot | Der Papagei, Die Papageien |
| Part | Der Teil, Die Teile |
| Parting | Der Abschied, Die Abschieden |
| Partner (mate) | Der Partner, Die Partner; Die Partnerin, Die Partnerinnen |
| Part-time Work | Die Teilzeitarbeit |
| Party (fun) | Die Party, Die Partys |
| Party (political) | Die Partei, Die Parteien |
| Pashto (language) | Das Paschtunisch |
| Passenger, Aviation, Nautical | Der Passagier, Die Passagiere; Die Passagierin, Die Passagierinnen |
| Passenger, Train, Taxi | Der Fahrgast, Die Fahrgäste |
| Passion, not passionate | Die Leidenschaft, Die Leidenschaften |
| Passport | Der Reisepass, Die Reisepässe |
| Past | Die Vergangenheit |
| Pastor | Der Pfarrer, Die Pfarrer; Die Pfarrerin, Die Pfarrerinnen |
| Pastry, Pastries | Das Gebäck |
| Path | Der Pfad, Die Pfade |
| Path, Way | Der Weg, Die Wege |
| Pathogen | Der Erreger, Die Erreger |
| Patience | Die Geduld |
| Pattern | Das Muster, Die Muster |
| Pause or Break | Die Pause, Die Pausen |
| Paw | Die Pfote, Die Pfoten |
| Payment | Die Zahlung, Die Zahlungen |

| English | German |
|---------|--------|
| Pea | Die Erbse, Die Erbsen |
| Peach | Der Pfirsich, Die Pfirsiche |
| Peak, Summit | Der Gipfel, Die Gipfel |
| Pear | Die Birne, Die Birnen |
| Pedestrian | Der Fußgänger, Die Fußgänger; Die Fußgängerin, Die Fußgängerinnen |
| Pedestrian Zone | Die Fußgängerzone, Die Fußgängerzonen |
| Pen (ballpoint) | Der Kugelschreiber, Die Kugelschreiber |
| Pen (ballpoint) | Der Kuli, Die Kulis |
| Penalty (sport) | Der Strafstoß, Die Strafstöße |
| Pencil (lead) | Der Bleistift, Die Bleistifte |
| Peninsula | Die Halbinsel, Die Halbinseln |
| People | Das Volk, Die Völker |
| Pepper | Das Pfeffer, Die Pfeffer |
| Pepper (bell) | Die Paprika, Die Paprikas |
| Percent | Das Prozent, Die Prozente |
| Perception | Die Wahrnehmung, Die Wahrnehmungen |
| Performance (art, play, opera) | Die Aufführung, Die Aufführungen |
| Persian (language) | Das Persisch |
| Person | Die Person, Die Personen |
| Personality | Die Persönlichkeit, Die Persönlichkeiten |
| Pet Store | Der Zooladen, Die Zooladen |
| Pharmacist | Der Apotheker, Die Apotheker; Die Apothekerin, Die Apothekerininnen |
| Pharmacy | Die Apotheke, Die Apotheken |
| Philosophy | Die Philosophie, Die Philosophien |
| Phone | Das Telefon, Die Telefone |
| Photo | Das Foto, Die Fotos |
| Physical Therapist | Der Physiotherapeut, Die Physiotherapeuten; Die Physiotherapeutin, Die Physiotherapeutinnen |
| Piano | Das Klavier, Die Klaviere |
| Piccolo | Die Piccoloflöte, Die Piccoloflöten |
| Picnic | Das Picknick, Die Picknicks |
| Picture | Das Bild, Die Bilder |
| Piece | Das Stück, Die Stücke |
| Pig | Das Schwein, Die Schweine |
| Pillow | Das Kissen, Die Kissen |
| Pilot | Der Pilot, Die Piloten; Die Politin, Die Pilotinnen |
| Pilsner | Das Pils, Die Pils |
| PIN (secret number) | Die Geheimzahl, Die Geheimzahlen |
| Pineapple | Die Ananas, Die Ananas |
| Pirate | Der Pirat, Die Piraten; Die Piratin, Die Piratinnen |
| Pisces | Die Fische |
| Pistol | Die Pistole, Die Pistolen |

| English | German |
|---|---|
| Pizza | Die Pizza, Die Pizzas |
| Place | Der Ort, Die Orte |
| Place | Der Platz, Die Plätze |
| Plan | Der Plan, Die Pläne |
| Plane Ticket | Die Flugkarte, Die Flugkarten |
| Planet | Der Planet, Die Planeten |
| Planning | Die Planung, Die Planungen |
| Plastic | Der Kunststoff, Die Kunststoff |
| Plate | Der Teller, Die Teller |
| Platform (train) | Der Bahnsteig, Die Bahnsteige |
| Pleasure | Die Freude, Die Freuden |
| Plum (oval, tart hybrid) | Die Zwetschge, Die Zwetschgen |
| Plum (round, sweet) | Die Pflaume, Die Pflaumen |
| Plumber | Der Klempner, Die Klempner |
| Pocket | Die Tasche, Die Taschen |
| Pocket (in a bag) | Das Fach, Die Fächer |
| Pocket Calculator | Der Taschenrechner, Die Taschenrechner |
| Poem | Das Gedicht, Die Gedichte |
| Poet | Der Dichter, Die Dichter |
| Point | Der Punkt, Die Punkte |
| Police | Die Polizei, Die Polizeien (plural is rare) |
| Policies (also see Regulation) | Die Regeln |
| Policy | Das Regeln, Die Regeln |
| Polish | Der Glanz |
| Polish (language) | Das Polnisch |
| Politician | Der Politiker, Die Politiker; Die Politikerin, Die Politikerinnen |
| Pollution (environment) | Die Umweltverschmutzung, Die Umweltverschmutzungen |
| Polygon | Das Polygon, Die Polygone |
| Pond | Der Teich, Die Teiche |
| Pool | Das Schwimmbecken, Die Pools |
| Popcorn | Das Popcorn |
| Pope | Der Papst, Die Päpste |
| Population | Die Bevölkerung, Die Bevölkerungen |
| Porch, Veranda | Die Veranda, Die Veranden |
| Porch, Vestibule | Die Vorhalle, Die Vorhallen |
| Pork | Das Schweinefleisch |
| Portal | Das Portal, Die Portale |
| Portion, Share (of something) | Der Anteil, Die Anteile |
| Portuguese (language) | Das Portugiesisch |
| Position (at work) | Die Stelle, Die Stellen |
| Position (stance) | Die Stellung, Die Stellungen |
| Position, Location | Die Lage, Die Lagen |

| English | German |
|---|---|
| Possibility | Die Möglichkeit, Die Möglichkeiten |
| Post Office | Das Postamt, Die Postämter |
| Pot (metal) | Der Topf, Die Töpfe |
| Potato | Die Kartoffel, Die Kartoffeln |
| Pound (British currency) | Das Pfund, Die Pfunde |
| Powdered Sugar | Der Puderzucker |
| Power, Force | Die Kraft, Die Kräfte |
| Practice (as in medical practice) | Die Praxis, Die Praktiken |
| Practice (to improve a skill) | Die Übung, Die Übungen |
| Prediction (forecast) | Die Vorhersage, Die Vorhersagen |
| Prediction (prophecy, like Nostradamus) | Die Voraussage, Die Voraussagen |
| Preferential Treatment | Die Vorzugsbehandlung, Die Vorzugsbehandlungen |
| Pregnancy | Die Schwangerschaft, Die Schwangerschaften |
| Preparation | Die Vorbereitung, Die Vorbereitungen |
| Prerequisites | Die Voraussetzung, Die Voraussetzungen |
| Presence | Die Anwesenheit |
| Present (time) | Die Gegenwart |
| President | Der Präsident, Die Präsidenten |
| Pressure, Stress | Der Druck |
| Pretzel | Die Brezel, Die Brezeln |
| Pricing | Die Preisgestaltung, Die Preisgestaltungen |
| Priest | Der Pfarrer, Die Pfarrer; Die Pfarrerin, Die Pfarrerinnen |
| Printer (machine) | Der Drucker, Die Drucker |
| Priority | Die Priorität, Die Prioritäten |
| Prison | Das Gefängnis, Die Gefängnisse |
| Problem | Das Problem, Die Probleme |
| Procedure, Method | Das Verfahren, Die Verfahren |
| Product (business) | Das Erzeugnis, Die Erzeugnisse |
| Product (goods) | Die Ware, Die Waren |
| Product (math) | Das Produkt, Die Produkte |
| Production | Die Herstellung, Die Herstellungen |
| Profession | Der Beruf, Die Berufe |
| Profit | Der Gewinn, Die Gewinne |
| Prognosis | Die Prognose, Die Prognosen |
| Progress, Advancement | Der Fortschritt, Die Fortschritte |
| Promotion (rank) | Die Beförderung, Die Beförderungen |
| Proof | Der Beweis, Die Beweise |
| Property | Das Eigentum, Die Eigentume |
| Prophet | Der Prophet, Die Propheten; Die Prophetin, Die Prophetinnen |

| English | German |
|---|---|
| Proposal, Suggestion | Der Vorschlag, Die Vorschläge |
| Prosecution | Die Anklage, Die Anklagen |
| Prosecutor | Der Ankläger, Die Ankläge; Die Anklägerin, Die Anklägerin |
| Protection, Shelter, Conservation | Der Schutz |
| Proton | Das Proton, Die Protonen |
| Psychology | Die Psychologie |
| Pterodactyl | Der Pterodactylus, Die Pterodactylen |
| Public | Die Öffentlichkeit |
| Public | Das Publikum |
| Publisher | Der Herausgeber, Die Herausgeber; Die Herausgeberin, Die Herausgeberinnen |
| Pumpkin | Die Kürbis, Die Kürbisse |
| Punishment, Penalty, Sentence | Die Strafe, Die Strafen |
| Puppy | Der Welpe, Die Welpen |
| Purchase | Der Einkauf, Die Einkäufe |
| Purpose, Function | Der Zweck, Die Zwecke |
| Quality | Die Qualität, Die Qualitäten |
| Quantity, Amount | Die Menge, Die Mengen |
| Queen | Die Königin, Die Königinnen |
| Quest, Search | Die Suche, Die Suchen |
| Question | Die Frage, Die Fragen |
| Quitting Time, End of Workday | Der Feierabend, Die Feierabende |
| Rabbit | Der Hase, Die Hasen |
| Rabbit | Das Kaninchen, Die Kaninchen |
| Race (sports) | Das Rennen, Die Rennen |
| Radio | Das Radio, Die Radios |
| Radio (receiver) | Der Radioempfänger, Die Radioempfänger |
| Radio (technical) | Der Funk |
| Radio Station | Die Funkstelle, Die Funkstellen |
| Rain | Der Regen, Die Regenzeit |
| Raincoat | Der Regenmantel, Die Regenmantäl |
| Raisin | Die Rosine, Die Rosinen |
| Raspberry | Die Himbeer, Die Himbeeren |
| Rat | Die Ratte, Die Ratten |
| Ratio, Proportion | Das Verhältnis, Die Verhältnisse |
| Ray | Der Strahl, Die Strahlen |
| Reaction, Response | Die Reaktion, Die Reaktionen |
| Reading | Die Lesung, Die Lesungen |
| Reality | Die Wirklichkeit, Die Wirklichkeiten |
| Reason | Der Grund, Die Gründe |

| English | German |
|---------|--------|
| Receipt | Die Quittung, Die Quittungen |
| Reception, Radio | Der Empfang, Die Empfänge |
| Recession | Die Rezession, Die Rezessionen |
| Recipe | Das Rezept, Die Rezepte |
| Recognition | Die Anerkennung, Die Anerkennungen |
| Record | Der Datensatz, Datensätze |
| Recording | Die Aufnahme, Die Aufnahmen |
| Recruitment | Die Anwerbung, Die Anwerbungen |
| Rectangle | Das Rechteck, Die Rechtecke |
| Red Cross | Das Rote Kreuz |
| Red Wine | Der Rotwein, Die Rotweine |
| Redeemer | Der Erlöser, Die Erlöser; Die Erlöserin, Die Erlöserinnen |
| Reference | Der Bezug, Die Bezüge |
| Reflection, Contemplation | Die Betrachtung, Die Betrachtungen |
| Reflection, Mirror Image | Das Spiegelbild, Die Spiegelbilder |
| Refrigerator | Der Kühlschrank, Die Kühlschränke |
| Refugee | Der Flüchtling, Die Flüchtlinge |
| Refutation | Die Verleugnung, Die Verleugnungen |
| Region | Das Gebiet, Die Gebiete |
| Registration (for a car, etc.) | Die Anmeldung, Die Anmeldungen |
| Registration Requirement | Die Anmeldpflicht, Die Anmeldpflichten |
| Regulation | Das Regeln, Die Regeln |
| Rejection | Die Ablehnung, Die Ablehnungen |
| Relationship | Die Beziehung, Die Beziehungen |
| Relative (family, next of kin) | Der Verwandte, Die Verwandten |
| Release (hostages) | Die Befreiung, Die Befreiungen |
| Religion | Die Religion, Die Religionen |
| Religious (usually an adjective) | no singular, Die Religiösen |
| Reminder | Die Erinnerung, Die Erinnerungen |
| Rent | Die Miete, Die Mieten |
| Rental Car | Der Mietwagen, Die Mietwagen |
| Report | Der Bericht, Die Berichte |
| Report | Das Zeugnis, Die Zeugnisse |
| Representation | Die Darstellung, Die Darstellungen |
| Republic | Die Republik, Die Republiken |
| Republic of the Congo | Der Kongo |
| Reputation | Das Ansehen |
| Request | Die Anfrage, Die Anfragen |
| Rescue | Die Rettung, Die Rettungen |
| Rescuer | Der Retter, Die Retter; Die Retterin, Die Reteterinnen |
| Research | Die Forschung, Die Forschungen |

| English | German |
|---|---|
| Resettlement | Die Umsiedlung, Die Umsiedlungen |
| Resident | Der Bewohner, Die Bewohner; Die Bewohnerin, Die Bewohnerinnen |
| Residents | Der Einwohner, Die Einwohner; Die Einwohnerin, Die Einwohnerinnen |
| Resistance | Der Widerstand, Die Widerstände |
| Resolution (determination) | Die Entschlusskraft, Die Entschlusskräfte |
| Resolution (resolved to disband) | Die Auflösung, Die Auflösungen |
| Responsibility | Die Verantwortung, Die Verantwortungen |
| Rest | Die Rast, Die Reste |
| Restaurant | Das Restaurant, Die Restaurants |
| Restoration | Die Wiederherstellung, Die Wiederherstellungen |
| Restraint | Die Zurückhaltung |
| Result | Das Ergebnis, Die Ergebnisse |
| Resume, CV | Der Lebenslauf, Die Lebensläufe |
| Retirement | Der Ruhestand |
| Return | Die Rückkehr |
| Revenue | Die Einnahme, Die Einnahmen |
| Reversal, Turning Back (for example, yield curve) | Die Umkehr |
| Revolution (per minute) | Die Umdrehung, Die Umdrehungen |
| Revolution (uprising) | Die Revolution, Die Revolutionen |
| Reward | Die Belohnung, Die Belohnungen |
| Rhinestone | Der Strass, Die Strasse |
| Rhinoceros | Das Nashorn, Die Nashörner |
| Rice | Der Reis |
| Right | Das Recht, Die Rechte |
| Ring | Der Ring, Die Ringe |
| Ringed Binder | Das Ringbuch, Die Ringbücher |
| Rise | Der Anstieg, Die Anstiege (from *anstiegen*) |
| Risk | Das Risk, Die Risken |
| River | Der Fluss, Die Flüsse |
| Road | Die Straße, Die Straßen |
| Robber | Der Räuber, Die Räuber; Die Räuberin, Die Räuberinnen |
| Rock | Der Fels, Die Felsen |
| Rocky Mountains | Die Rocky Mountains |
| Role (theater, not function) | Die Rolle, Die Rollen |
| Rolling Pin | Das Nudelholz, Die Nudelhölzer |
| Romanian (language) | Das Rumänisch |
| Romantic | Der Romantiker, Die Romantiker; Die Romantikerin, Die Romantikerinnen |
| Romanticism | Die Romantik |

| English | German |
|---------|--------|
| Roof | Das Dach, Die Dächer |
| Room | Das Zimmer, Die Zimmer |
| Room (space) | Die Raum, Die Räume |
| Roommate | Der Mitbewohner, Die Mitbewohner; Die Mitbewohnerin, Die Mitbewohnerinnen |
| Rooster | Der Hahn, Die Hähne |
| Root | Die Wurzel, Die Wurzeln |
| Rose | Die Rose, Die Rosen |
| Roundtrip | Die Rundfahrt, Die Rundfahrten |
| Row | Die Reihe, Die Reihen |
| Rowboat | Das Ruderboot, Die Ruderboote |
| Rum | Der Rum, Die Rums |
| Runway (airport) | Die Landebahn, Die Landebahnen |
| Russian (language) | Das Russisch |
| Rye | Der Roggen |
| Rye Whiskey | Der Rye, Der Roggenwhisky, Die Roggenwhiskys |
| Sacrament | Das Sakrament, Die Sakramente |
| Sadism | Der Sadismus |
| Sadist | Der Sadist, Die Sadisten; Die Sadistin, Die Sadistinnen |
| Safety | Die Sicherheit |
| Sagittarius | Der Schütze, Die Schützen |
| Saint | Der Heilige, Die Heiligen |
| Salad | Der Salat, Die Salate |
| Salaried, White-Collar Employee | Der Angestellte, Die Angestellten; Die Angestellte, Die Angestellten |
| Salary | Das Gehalt, Die Gehälter |
| Sales, Turnover | Der Umsatz, Die Umsätze |
| Salmon | Der Lachs, Die Lachse |
| Salt | Das Salz, Die Salze |
| Sample (food) | Die Kostprobe, Die Kostproben |
| Sand | Der Sand, Der Sand |
| Satisfaction | Die Zufriedenheit |
| Saturday | Der Samstag, Die Samstage |
| Saturday | Der Sonnabend, Die Sonnabende |
| Sauce, Gravy | Die Soße, Die Soßen |
| Sausage | Die Wurst, Die Würste |
| Savior | Der Erretter, Die Erretter; Die Erretterin, Die Erretterinnen |
| Saxophone | Das Saxaphon, Die Saxaphone |
| Scale (to weigh) | Die Waage, Die Waagen |
| Scallop | Die Jakobsmuschel, Die Jakobsmuscheln |
| Scarf | Der Schal, Die Schals |
| Scenario | Das Szenario, Die Szenarien |

| English | German |
|---------|--------|
| Scene | Die Szene, Die Szenen |
| Schnaps | Der Schnaps |
| School Bus | Der Schulbus, Die Schulbusse |
| Science | Die Wissenschaft, Die Wissenschaften |
| Scissor | Die Schere, Die Scheren |
| Scorpio | Der Skorpion, Die Skorpione |
| Scotch | Der Scotch, Die Scotchs |
| Scrambled Egg | Das Rührei, Die Rühreier |
| Screen | Der Bildschirm, Die Bildschirme |
| Scripture | Die Schrift, Die Schriften |
| Sea | Die See, Die Seen |
| Sea | Das Meer, Die Meere |
| Seafood (on menus) | Die Meeresfrüchte |
| Seagull | Die Möwe, Die Möwen |
| Season (for sport, theater, etc.) | Die Saison, Die Saisons |
| Season (of the year) | Die Jahreszeit, Die Jahreszeiten |
| Seat | Der Sitzplatz, Die Sitzplätze |
| Second | Der Zweite, Die Zweiten |
| Second (time) | Die Sekunde, Die Sekunden |
| Secret | Das Geheimnis, Die Geheimnisse |
| Secretary | Der Sekretär, Die Sekretäre; Die Sekretärin, Die Sekretärinnen |
| Seller | Der Verkäufer, Die Verkäufer; Die Verkäuferin, Die Verkäuferinnen |
| Semester | Das Semester, Die Semester |
| Semi-conductor | Der Halbleiter, Die Halbleiter |
| Senate | Der Senat, Die Senate |
| Senator | Der Senator, Die Senatoren; Die Senatorin, Die Senatorinnen |
| Sentence | Der Satz, Die Sätze |
| Separation | Die Trennung, Die Trennungen |
| September | Der September |
| Serbian (language) | Das Serbisch |
| Service | Der Dienst, Die Dienste |
| Setting | Die Einstellung, Die Einstellungen |
| Settlement | Die Siedlung, Die Siedlungen |
| Sewage | Das Abwasser |
| Shadow | Der Schatten, Die Schatten |
| Shape | Die Form, Die Formen |
| Shape, Form | Die Gestalt, Die Gestalte |
| Shareholder | Der Anteilseigner, Die Anteilseigner; Die Anteilseignerin, Die Anteilseignerinnen |
| Shark | Der Hai, Die Haie |

| English | German |
|---|---|
| Shark, Hammerhead | Der Hammerhai, Die Hammerhaie |
| Sheep | Die Schafe |
| Sheet | Das Blatt, Die Blätter |
| Sheet Metal | Das Blech, Die Bleche |
| Shelf | Das Regal, Die Regale |
| Shellfish | Das Schalentier, Die Schalentiere |
| Shelling | Der Beschuss |
| Shepheard | Der Schäfer, Die Schäfer; Die Schäferin, Die Schäferinnen |
| Shield (that a warrior carries) | Der Schild, Die Schilde (different from Das Schild) |
| Shift Work | Die Schichtarbeit, Die Schichtarbeiten |
| Shine, Sheen | Der Glanz |
| Ship | Das Schiff, Die Schiffe |
| Shirt | Das Hemd, Die Hemden |
| Shit | Die Scheiße, Die Scheiße |
| Shock | Der Schock, Die Schocks |
| Shoe | Der Schuh, Die Schuhe |
| Shoe Polish | Die Schuhcreme, Die Schuhcremes |
| Shoe Store | Der Schuhladen, Die Schuhladen |
| Shoelace | Der Schnürsenkel, Die Schnürsenkel |
| Shop, Store | Das Geschäft, Die Geschäfte |
| Shopping Bag | Die Einkaufstasche, Die Einkaufstaschen |
| Shot (gun shot or shot on goal) | Der Schuss, Die Schüsse |
| Shoulder | Die Schulter, Die Schultern |
| Show | Die Show, Die Shows |
| Shower | Die Dusche, Die Duschen |
| Shrimp | Die Garnele, Die Garnelen |
| Side | Die Seite, Die Seiten |
| Sideline (sport) | Die Seitenlinie, Die Seitenlinien |
| Sidewalk | Der Bürgersteig, Die Bürgersteige |
| Sight (as in "see the sights") | Die Sehenswürdigkeit, Die Sehenswürdigkeiten |
| Sign (graphic, drawn) | Die Zeichen, Die Zeichen |
| Sign, Plate (road) | Das Schild, Die Schilder (different from Der Schild) |
| Signature | Die Unterschrift, Die Unterschriften |
| Silence | Die Stille, Die Stille |
| Silver | Das Silber, Die Silber |
| Silver Coin | Die Silbermünze, Die Silbermünzen |
| Silver Medal | Die Silbermedaille, Die Silbermedaillen |
| Silverware | Das Tafelsilber |
| Singer | Der Sänger, Die Sänger; Die Sängerin, Die Sängerinnen |
| Single Room | Das Einzelzimmer, Die Einzelzimmer |
| Sister | Die Schwester, Die Schwestern |

145

| English | German |
|---------|--------|
| Situation | Die Lage, Die Lagen |
| Size, Magnitude | Die Größe, Die Größen |
| Skin | Die Haut, Die Häute |
| Skirt | Der Rock, Die Röcke |
| Sky, Heaven | Der Himmel, Der Himmel |
| Skyscraper | Der Wolkenkratzer, Die Wolkenkratzer |
| Sleep | Der Schlaf |
| Slovakia | Die Slowakei |
| Smell | Der Geruch, Die Gerüche |
| Smile | Das Lächeln, Die Lächeln |
| Smoke | Der Rauch |
| Snake | Die Schlange, Die Schlangen |
| Sneaker | Der Turnschuh, Die Turnschuhe |
| Snow | Der Schnee |
| Soccer | Der Fußball, Die Fußbälle |
| Soccer Goal | Das Fußballtor, Die Fußballtore |
| Soccer Net | Das Tornetz, Die Tornetze |
| Society | Die Gesellschaft, Die Gesellschaften |
| Sock | Die Socke, Die Socken |
| Software | Die Software, Die Softwares |
| Soil | Der Erdboden, Die Erdböden; Die Erde, Die Erden |
| Soldier | Der Soldat, Die Soldaten |
| Solution | Die Lösungen, Die Lösungen |
| Son | Der Sohn, Die Söhne |
| Song | Der Sang, Die Sänge |
| Song | Das Lied, Die Lieder |
| Soprano | Der Sopranist, Die Sopranisten; Die Sopranistin, Die Sopranistinnen |
| Soul | Die Seele, Die Seelen |
| Sound (harmonies) | Der Klang |
| Sound (non-musical) | Das Geräusch, Die Geräusche |
| Soup | Die Suppe, Die Suppen |
| Source | Die Quelle, Die Quellen |
| South | Der Süden, Die Souths |
| Soy | Die Soja, Die Sojen |
| Space (astronomy) | Der Raum, Die Räume |
| Spatula | Der Pfannenwender (or Der Wender), Die Pfannenwender |
| Special Offers | Die Sonderangebot, Die Sonderangebote |
| Speech, Address | Die Rede, Die Reden |
| Speed | Die Geschwindigkeit, Die Geschwindigkeiten |
| Speed Limit | Die Geschwindigkeitsbegrenzung, Die Geschwindigkeitsbegrenzungen |

| English | German |
| --- | --- |
| Spice, Seasoning | Das Gewürz, Die Gewürze |
| Spider | Die Spinne, Die Spinnen |
| Spirit | Der Geist, Die Geister |
| Spirit, in the | im Geiste |
| Sponge | Der Schwamm, Die Schwämme |
| Spool, Reel | Die Spule, Die Spulen |
| Spoon | Der Löffel, Die Löffel |
| Sport Coat | Das Sakko, Die Sakkos |
| Spot | Der Fleck, Die Flecken |
| Spring | Der Frühling |
| Spring | Das Frühjahr |
| Spy | Der Spion, Die Spione; Die Spionin, Die Spioninnen |
| Square | Das Quadrat, Die Quadräte |
| Squeezer | Die Presse, Die Pressen |
| Squid | Der Tintenfisch |
| Squirrel | Das Eichhörnchen, Die Eichhörnchen |
| Stability | Die Stabilität, Die Stabilitäten |
| Stadium | Die Stadion, Die Stadien |
| Staff | Das Personal |
| Stage | Die Bühne, Die Bühnen |
| Stain | Der Fleck, Die Flecken |
| Stair | Die Treppe, Die Treppen |
| Stallion | Der Hengst, Die Hengste |
| Star | Der Stern, Die Sterne |
| State (Bavaria, Florida, etc.) | Der Staat, Die Staaten |
| State (within the US) | Der US-Bundesstaat, Die US-Bundesstaaten |
| State Attorney | Der Staatsanwalt, Die Staatsanwälte; Die Staatsanwältin, Die Staatsanwältinnen |
| State President, Governor | Der Staatspräsident, Die Staatspräsidenten; Die Staatspräsidentin, Die Staatspräsidentinnen |
| Station (transit) | Die Station, Die Stationen |
| Statue | Die Statue, Die Statuen |
| Steak | Das Steak, Die Steaks |
| Steering Wheel | Das Lenkrad, Die Lenkräder |
| Step | Der Schritt, Die Schritte |
| Stepchild | Das Stiefkind, Die Stiefkinder |
| Stepdaughter | Die Stieftochter, Die Stieftöchter |
| Stepson | Der Stiefsohn, Die Stiefsöhne |
| Stew | Der Eintopf, Die Eintöpfe |
| Sting, Prick, Stab | Der Stich, Die Stiche |
| Stock Exchange | Die Börse, Die Börsen |
| Stock Market | Der Aktienmarkt, Die Aktienmärkte |
| Stock Option | Die Aktienoption, Die Aktienoptionen |

| English | German |
|---|---|
| Stomach | Der Magen, Die Mägen |
| Stone | Der Stein, Die Steine |
| Stop Sign | Das Stoppschild, Die Stoppschilder |
| Stoplight, Traffic Light | Die Ampel, Die Ampeln |
| Storage | Die Lagerung, Die Lagerungen |
| Storage (memory, attic) | Der Speicher, Die Speicher |
| Store, Shop | Der Laden, Die Laden |
| Storm | Der Sturm, Die Stürme |
| Story (spoken story, narration) | Die Erzählung, Die Erzählungen |
| Story (tale) | Die Geschichte, Die Geschichten |
| Stove | Der Herd, Die Herde |
| Stranger | Der Fremde, Die Fremden |
| Strategy (general, civilian) | Die Strategie, Die Strategien |
| Strategy (military) | Die Kriegskunst |
| Straw | Das Stroh |
| Strawberry | Die Erdbeere, Die Erdbeeren |
| Street | Die Straße, Die Straßen |
| Stress | Der Stress |
| Stretch (of road) | Die Strecke, Die Strecken |
| Strike, Walkout | Der Streik, Die Streike |
| String (instrument) | Die Saite, Die Saiten |
| String, Cord | Die Schnur, Die Schnüre |
| Struggle | Der Kampf, Die Kämpfe |
| Student | Der Schüler, Die Studenten |
| Studio | Das Studio, Die Studios |
| Stuff | Das Zeug, Die Stoffe |
| Stumbling Block | Der Hemmschuh, Die Hemmschuhe |
| Sturm und Drang/Storm and Stress (German literary movement, 18th Century) | Der Sturm und Drang |
| Subject (a discipline of study or a department) | Das Fach, Die Fäche |
| Subsistence | Die Verpflegung, Die Verpflegungen |
| Subtitle | Der Untertitel, Die Untertitel |
| Success | Der Erfolg, Die Erfolge |
| Sudan | Der Sudan |
| Suffering | Das Leiden, Die Leiden |
| Sugar | Der Zucker |
| Sugar Cube | Der Zuckerwürfel, Die Zuckerwürfel |
| Suit | Der Anzug, Die Anzüge |
| Suitcase | Der Koffer, Die Koffer |
| Summer | Der Sommer, Die Sommer |
| Sun | Die Sonne, Die Sonnen |

| English | German |
|---------|--------|
| Sunday | Der Sonntag, Die Sonntage |
| Sunrise | Der Sonnenaufgang, Die Sonnenaufgänge |
| Sunset | Der Sonnenuntergang, Die Sonnenuntergänge |
| Superiority | Die Überlegenheit, Die Überlegenheiten |
| Supermarket | Der Supermarkt, Die Supermärkte |
| Supervisor | Der Vorgesetzter, Die Vorgesetzten; Die Vorgesetzte, Die Vorgesetzten |
| Supply, Inventory | Der Vorrat, Die Vorräte |
| Supporter, Backer | Der Anhänger, Die Anhänger; Die Anhängerin, Die Anhängerinnen |
| Supporter, Endorser | Der Unterstützer, Die Unterstützer; Die Unterstützerin, Die Unterstützerinnen |
| Suppression, Oppression | Die Unterdrückung, Die Unterdrückungen |
| Surface | Die Oberfläche, Die Oberflächen |
| Surfboard | Das Surfbrett, Die Surfbretter |
| Surgeon | Der Chirug, Die Chirugen; Die Chirugerin, Die Chirugerinnen |
| Surprise | Die Überraschung, Die Überraschungen |
| Suspect | Der Verdächtige, Die Verdächtigen; Die Verdächtige, Die Verdächtigen |
| Suspension | Die Abhängung, Die Abhängungen |
| Swahili (language) | Das Swahili |
| Sweater | Der Pulli, Die Pullis |
| Swedish (language) | Das Schwedisch |
| Sweet Potato | Die Süßkartoffel, Die Süßkartoffeln |
| Sweets (not baked) | no singular, Die Süßigkeiten |
| Swimming Pool | Das Schwimmbad, Die Schwimmbäder |
| Swimming Trunks | Die Badehosen |
| Switzerland | Die Schweiz |
| Sword | Das Schwert, Die Schwerter |
| Swordfish | Der Schwertfisch |
| System | Das System, Die Systems |
| Table | Der Tisch, Die Tische |
| Table (data) | Das Tabellenwerk, Die Tabellenwerke |
| Tablespoon | Der Esslöffel, Die Esslöffeln |
| Tagalog (language) | Das Tagalog |
| Tariff, Customs, Levy, Toll | Der Zoll, Die Zölle |
| Tarragon | Der Estragon |
| Task | Der Auftrag, Die Aufträge |
| Task | Die Aufgabe, Die Aufgaben |
| Taurus | Der Stier, Die Stiere |
| Tavern | Das Wirtshaus, Die Wirtshäuser |
| Tax | Die Steuer, Die Steuern |
| Taxi | Das Taxi, Die Taxis |

| English | German |
|---|---|
| Taxi Driver | Der Taxifahrer, Die Taxifahrer; Die Taxifahrerin, Die Taxifahrerinnen |
| Tea | Der Tee, Die Tees |
| Teacher | Der Lehrer, Die Lehrer; Die Lehrerin, Die Lehrerinnen |
| Team | Die Manschaft, Die Mannschaften (also Das Team) |
| Team | Das Team, Die Teams |
| Tear (crying) | Die Träne, Die Tränen |
| Teaspoon | Der Teelöffel, Die Teelöffeln |
| Technology | Die Technologie, Die Technologien |
| Teetotaler | Der Abstinenzler, Die Abstinenzler; Die Abstinenzlerin, Die Abstinenzlerinnen |
| Television | Das Fernseher, Die Fernseher |
| Template, Model | Die Vorlage, Die Vorlagen |
| Tempo | Das Tempo, Die Tempi, Die Tempos |
| Tennis | Das Tennis |
| Tennis Match | Das Tennisspiel, Die Tennisspiele |
| Tenor | Der Tenor, Die Tenöre |
| Term (in office) | Die Amtszeit, Die Amtszeiten |
| Terrorism | Der Terrorismus |
| Terrorist | Der Terrorist, Die Terroristen; Die Terroristin, Die Terroristinnen |
| Terrorist Attack | Der Terroranschlag, Die Terroränschlage |
| Test (school, verification) | Die Prüfung, Die Prüfungen |
| Text Message | Die SMS-Nachricht (or just Die SMS), Die SMS-Nachrichten |
| Texture, Arrangement | Das Gefüge, Die Gefüge |
| Thanks | Der Dank |
| The Fifth | Der Fünfte |
| The First | Der Erste |
| The Fourth | Der Vierte |
| The Second | Der Dritte |
| The Seventh | Der Siebente |
| The Sixth | Der Sechste |
| The Thirty-first | Der Einunddreißigste |
| Theater | Das Theater, Die Theater |
| Theory | Die Theorie, Die Theorien |
| Thief | Der Dieb, Die Dieben; Die Diebin, Die Diebinnen |
| Thimble | Der Fingerhut, Die Fingerhüte |
| Thing | Das Ding, Die Dinge |
| Thorn | Der Stachel, Die Stacheln |
| Thought | Der Gedanke, Die Gedanken |
| Threat | Die Drohung, Die Drohungen |
| Thrust, Boost | Der Schube, Die Schübe |

| English | German |
|---|---|
| Thumb | Der Daumen, Die Daumen |
| Thunder | Der Donner, Die Donner |
| Thunderstorm | Das Gewitter, Die Gewitter |
| Thursday | Der Donnerstag, Die Donnerstage |
| Tick (insect) | Die Zecke, Die Zecken |
| Ticket | Das Ticket, Die Tickets |
| Ticket (for train or bus) | Die Fahrkarte, Die Fahrkarten |
| Ticket Vending Machine | Der Fahrkartenautomat, Die Fahrkartenautomaten |
| Tie, Draw (sports) | Die Auslosung, Die Auslosungen |
| Tiger | Der Tiger, Die Tiger |
| Time | Die Zeit, Die Zeiten |
| Timepoint | Das Mal, Die Male |
| Timer | Der Kurzzeitwecker, Die Kurzzeitwecker |
| Tire | Der Reifen, Die Reifen |
| Tire (flat) | Die Panne, Die Pannen |
| Tire, Car | Der Autoreifen, Die Autoreifen |
| Title (book, film) | Der Titel, Die Titel |
| Title (job) | Die Berufsbezeichnung, Die Berufsbezeichnungen |
| Tone (sine wave) | Der Ton, Die Töne |
| Tongs | Die Zange, Die Zangen |
| Tongue | Die Zunge, Die Zungen |
| Tool | Der Werkzeug, Die Werkzeuge |
| Tooth | Der Zahn, Die Tooths |
| Toothache | Der Zahnschmerz, Die Zahnschmerzen |
| Top | Die Spitze, Die Spitzen |
| Topic | Das Thema, Die Themen |
| Tornado | Der Tornado, Die Tornados |
| Towel (bath) | Das Badetuch, Die Badetücher |
| Towel (hand) | Das Handtuch, Die Handtücher |
| Town | Die Stadt, Die Städte |
| Toy | Das Spielzeug, Die Spielzeuge |
| Trade, Deal (economic) | Der Handel |
| Tradition | Die Tradition, Die Traditionen |
| Train | Der Zug, Die Züge |
| Train Station | Der Bahnhof, Die Bahnhöfe |
| Transformation | Das Veränderung, Die Veränderungen |
| Translation | Die Übersetzung, Die Übersetzungen |
| Trash | Der Müll |
| Traveler | Der Reisende, Die Reisenden; Die Reisende, Die Reisenden |
| Treatment | Die Behandlung, Die Behandlungen |
| Tree | Der Baum, Die Bäume |
| Trial | Der Prozess, Die Prozesse |
| Triangle | Das Dreieck, Die Dreiecke |

| English | German |
|---------|--------|
| Trip | Die Reise, Die Reisen |
| Trombone | Die Posaune, Die Posaunen |
| Troop | Die Truppe, Die Truppen |
| Trophy Cup | Der Pokal, Die Pokale |
| Trout | Die Forelle, Die Forellen |
| Truck | Der Lastkraftwagen (Lkw), Die Lastkraftwagen |
| Trumpet | Die Trompete, Die Trompeten |
| Truth | Die Wahrheit, Die Wahrheiten |
| Tuesday | Der Dienstag, Die Dienstage |
| Tuna | Der Thunfisch, Die Thunfische |
| Turkey | Die Türkei |
| Turkish (language) | Das Türkisch |
| Turn | Die Wende, Die Windungen |
| Turn Signal | Der Blinker, Die Blinker |
| Turtle | Die Schildkröte, Die Schildkröten |
| Twig (tree) | Der Zweig, Die Zweige |
| Twin | Der Zwilling, Die Zwillinge |
| Tycoon | Der Tycoon, Die Tycoons |
| Type | Die Art, Die Arten |
| Type (colloquially a fellow, guy) | Der Typ, Die Typen |
| Ukrainian (language) | Das Ukrainisch |
| Umbrella | Der Regenschirm, Die Regenschirme |
| Uncle | Der Onkel, Die Onkel |
| Understanding, Insight | Das Verständnis, Die Verständnisse |
| Underwear | Die Unterwäsche, Die Unterkleidung |
| Unemployed | Der Arbeitslose, Die Arbeitslosen |
| Unemployment | Die Arbeitslosigkeit |
| Unit (military) | Die Einheit, Die Einheiten |
| Unit (of measure) | Die Maßeinheit, Die Maßeinheiten |
| United Arab Emirates | Die Vereinigten Arabischen Emirate |
| United States | Die Vereinigten Staaten, Die USA |
| Unity | Die Einigkeit |
| Universe | Das All |
| University | Die Universität, Die Universitäten |
| Unknown (the unknown, not a person) | Das Unbekannte, Die Unbekannten |
| Urge, Compulsion | Der Drang, Die Dränge |
| Use, Input | Der Einsatz, Die Einsätze |
| User | Der Benutzer, Die Benutzer; Die Benutzerin, Die Benutzerinnen |
| Vacation | Der Urlaub, Die Urlaube (plural is rare) |
| Value | Der Wert, Die Werte |
| Variety | Die Sorte, Die Sorten |

| English | German |
|---|---|
| Vatican City | Der Vatikan |
| Vegetable | Das Gemüse, Die Gemüse |
| Vehicle | Das Fahrzeug, Die Fahrzeuge |
| Velocity | Die Schnelle, Die Schnellen |
| Vending Machine | Der Automat, Die Automaten |
| Venture, Undertaking (economic) | Das Unternehmen, Die Unternehmen |
| Verb | Das Verb, Die Verben |
| Version | Die Version, Die Versionen |
| Vessel (kitchen) | Das Gefäß, Die Gefäße |
| Victim | Das Opfer, Die Opfer |
| Victory | Der Sieg, Die Siege |
| Video | Das Video, Die Videos |
| View | Die Aussicht, Die Ansichten |
| View, Gaze, Look | Der Blick, Die Blicke |
| View, Opinion | Die Auffassung, Die Auffassenungen |
| Viewing, Visual Inspection | Die Besichtigung, Die Besichtigungen |
| Village | Das Dorf, Die Dörfer |
| Village Idiot | Der Dorfdepp, Die Dorfdeppen |
| Viola | Die Bratsche, Die Bratschen |
| Violence | Die Gewalt, Die Gewalten |
| Violin | Die Geige, Die Geigen |
| Virgo | Die Jungfrau, Die Jungfrauen |
| Virtue, Benefit, Value, Merit | Die Vorzug, Die Vorzüge |
| Virus | Das Virus, Die Viren |
| Vision | Die Vision, Die Visionen |
| Visit | Der Besuch, Die Besuche |
| Vocabulary | Der Wortschatz, Die Wortschätze |
| Vodka | Der Wodka, Die Wodkas |
| Voice, Vote | Die Stimme, Die Stimmen |
| Volume (audio) | Die Lautstärke, Die Lautstärken |
| Vote (between choices) | Die Wahl, Die Wahlen |
| Vote (choosing a direction, process) | Die Abstimmung, Die Abstimmungen |
| Voter | Der Wähler, Die Wähler; Die Wählerin, Die Wählerinnen |
| Wage | Der Lohn, Die Löhne |
| Wage, Pay, Earnings | Das Gehalt, Die Gehälter |
| Walk | Der Spaziergang, Die Spaziergänge |
| Wall (as in the Berlin Wall, etc.) | Die Mauer, Die Mauern |
| Wall (inside) | Die Wand, Die Wände |
| Wallet | Der Geldbeutel, Die Geldbeutel |
| War | Der Krieg, Die Kriege |

| English | German |
|---------|--------|
| Warning | Die Warnung, Die Warnungen |
| Washcloth | Der Waschlappen, Die Waschlappen |
| Wasp | Die Wespe, Die Wespen |
| Water | Das Wasser, Die Wasser |
| Watermelon | Die Wassermelone, Die Wassermelonen |
| Wave | Die Welle, Die Wellen |
| Wax | Das Wachs, Die Wachse |
| Way | Der Weg, Die Wege |
| Weakness | Die Schwäche, Die Schwächen |
| Wealth | Der Reichtum, Die Reichtümer |
| Weapon | Die Waffe, Die Waffen |
| Weather | Das Wetter |
| Weather Forecast | Die Wettervorhersagen, Die Wettervorhersagen |
| Website | Die Website, Die Websites |
| Wedding | Die Hochzeit, Die Hochzeiten |
| Wedding Reception | Die Hochzeitparty, Die Hochzeitpartys |
| Wedding Ring | Der Ehering, Die Eheringe |
| Wednesday | Der Mittwoch, Die Mittwochen |
| Week | Die Woche, Die Wochen |
| Weekend | Das Wochenende, Die Wochenenden |
| Weight | Das Gewicht, Die Gewichte |
| Welsh (language) | Das Walisisch |
| West | Der Westen |
| Wheat | Der Weizen |
| Wheat Beer | Das Weizenbier, Die Weizenbiere |
| Wheel | Das Rad, Die Räder |
| Whisk | Der Schneebesen, Die Schneebesen |
| Whiskey | Der Whisky, Die Whiskys |
| Whistle, Final | Der Abpfiff, Die Abpfiffe |
| White Wine | Der Weißwein, Die Weißweine |
| Wholesaler | Der Großhändler, Die Großhändler; Die Großhändlerin, Die Großhändlerinnen |
| Widow | Die Witwe, Die Witwen |
| Widower | Der Witwer, Die Witwer |
| Wife | Die Ehefrau, Die Ehefrauen |
| Wife | Die Frau, Die Frauen |
| Will (inner commitment) | Der Wille, Die Willen |
| Wind | Der Wind, Die Winde |
| Window | Das Fenster, Die Fenster |
| Windshield | Die Windschutzscheibe, Die Windschutzscheiben |
| Windshield Wiper | Der Scheibenwischer, Die Scheibenwischer |
| Windstorm | Der Sturm, Die Stürme |
| Wine | Der Wein, Die Weine |
| Wing | Der Flügel, Die Flügel |

| English | German |
|---|---|
| Winner | Der Gewinner, Die Gewinner; Die Gewinnerin, Die Gewinnernnen |
| Winter | Der Winter, Die Winter |
| Woman | Die Frau, Die Frauen |
| Wood (woodwork) | Das Holz |
| Wood, tree grouping | Der Wald, Die Wälder |
| Word | Das Wort, Die Wörter |
| Work | Die Arbeit, Die Werke |
| Work Accident | Der Arbeitsunfall, Die Arbeitsunfälle |
| Workday | Der Werktag, Die Werktagen |
| Worker, Laborer, Blue-Collar Employee | Der Arbeiter, Die Arbeiter; Die Arbeiterin, Die Arbeiterinnen |
| World | Die Welt, Die Welt |
| Worldview, Ideology | Die Weltanschauung, Die Weltanschauungen |
| Worry, Concern | Die Sorge, Die Sorgen |
| Writing | Die Schrift, Die Schriften |
| Writing Utensil (any type) | Der Stift, Die Stifte |
| X-Ray | Das Röntgen |
| Yacht | Die Jacht, Die Jachten |
| Yankee | Der Yankee, Die Yankees |
| Yard | Der Hof, Die Höfe |
| Yarn | Das Garn, Die Garne |
| Yawn | Das Gähnen |
| Year | Das Jahr, Die Jahre |
| Yearbook | Das Jahrbuch, Die Jahrbücher |
| Yeast | Die Hefe, Die Hefen |
| Yemen | Der Jemen |
| Yield, Gain (agriculture) | Der Ertrag, Die Erträge |
| Yoga | Das Yoga |
| Young Man, Boy | Der Junge, Die Jungen |
| Zealot, Fanatic | Der Fanatiker, Die Fanatiker; Die Fanatikerin, Die Fanatikerinnen |
| Zebra | Das Zebra, Die Zebras |
| Zipper | Der Reißverschluss, Die Reißverschlüsse |
| Zodiac | Der Tierkreis, Die Tierkreise |
| Zodiac Sign | Das Sternzeichen, Die Sternzeichen |
| Zone | Die Zone, Die Zonen |
| Zoo | Der Tiergarten, Die Tiergärten |
| Zoo | Der Tierpark, Die Tierparks |
| Zoo | Der Zoo, Die Zoos |
| Zucchini | Die Zucchini, Die Zucchini |

# 14

# PROPER AND SPECIAL NOUNS

## DAYS, MONTHS, AND SEASONS

Each day of the week has a singular version and two plural versions. The plurals that end with -e are countable, as in *Manchmal gibt es 52 Sonntage in einem Jahr* (*There are sometimes 52 Sundays in a year*), while the plurals that end with -s are not, as in *Ich gehe Sonntags zu meinen Eltern* (*I go to my parents on Sundays*). The -s ending can also be used to make the plural *Morgens*, as in *Morgens trinke ich gern Kaffee* (*In the mornings I like to drink coffee*). When you count a thing's position, the ordinal numbers (first, second, third, etc.), as in *der erste Tag* (*the first day*), are adjectives and take the adjective ending of the definite or indefinite article.

### *DAYS*

| English | German |
|---|---|
| Sunday | Der Sonntag, Die Sonntage, Sonntags |
| Monday | Der Montag, Die Montage, Montags |
| Tuesday | Der Dienstag, Die Dienstage, Dienstags |
| Wednesday | Der Mittwoch, Die Mittwoche, Mittwochs |
| Thursday | Der Donnerstag, Die Donnerstage, Donnerstags |
| Friday | Der Freitag, Die Freitage, Freitags |
| Saturday | Der Samstag, Die Samstage, Samstags |
| | Der Sonnabend, Die Sonnabende, Sonnabends |

### *MONTHS*

| English | German |
|---|---|
| January | Der Januar |
| February | Der Februar |
| March | Der März |
| April | Der April |

156

| English | German |
|---|---|
| May | Der Mai |
| June | Der Juni |
| July | Der Juli |
| August | Der August |
| September | Der September |
| October | Der Oktober |
| November | Der November |
| December | Der Dezember |

## SEASONS

| English | German |
|---|---|
| Spring | Der Frühling, Das Frühjahr |
| Summer | Der Sommer, Die Sommer |
| Autumn | Der Herbst, Die Herbste |
| Winter | Der Winter, Die Winter |

# LANGUAGES, COUNTRIES, AND REGIONS

## LANGUAGES

Languages have no plurals.

| English | German | English | German |
|---|---|---|---|
| Arabic | Das Arabisch | Japanese | Das Japanisch |
| Aramaic | Das Aramäisch | Korean | Das Koreanisch |
| Armenian | Das Armenisch | Kurdish | Das Kurdisch |
| Bulgarian | Das Bulgarisch | Latin | Das Latein |
| Chinese | Das Chinesisch | Latvian | Das Lettisch |
| Czech | Das Tschechisch | Lithuanian | Das Litauisch |
| Danish | Das Dänisch | Mandarin | Das Mandarin |
| Dutch | Das Niederländisch | Norwegian | Das Norwegisch |
| English | Das Englisch | Pashto | Das Paschtunisch |
| Estonian | Das Estnisch | Persian | Das Persisch |
| Finnish | Das Finnisch | Polish | Das Polnisch |
| French | Das Französisch | Portuguese | Das Portugiesisch |
| Frisian | Das Friesisch | Romanian | Das Rumänisch |
| Gaelic | Das Gälisch | Russian | Das Russisch |
| German | Das Deutsch | Serbian | Das Serbisch |
| Greek | Das Griechisch | Swahili | Das Swahili |
| Hebrew | Das Hebräisch | Swedish | Das Schwedisch |
| Hindi | Das Hindi | Tagalog | Das Tagalog |
| Hungarian | Das Ungarisch | Turkish | Das Türkisch |
| Icelandic | Das Isländisch | Ukrainian | Das Ukrainisch |
| Italian | Das Italienisch | Welsh | Das Walisisch |

## COUNTRIES AND REGIONS

In German, some nations have articles, either masculine or feminine, like *die Türkei, der Vatikan, die Vereinigte Staaten*, and *die Schweiz*, but most do not.

| English | German |
|---|---|
| Algeria | Algerien |
| Argentina | Argentinien |
| Aruba | Aruba |
| Australia | Australien |
| Austria | Österreich |
| Bahamas | Bahamas |
| Belarus | Weißrussland |
| Belgium | Belgien |
| Brazil | Brasilien |
| California | Kalifornien |
| Cameroon | Kamerun |
| Canada | Kanada |
| Chad | Tschad |
| Corsica | Korsika |
| Cuba | Kuba |
| Democratic Republic of the Congo | Die Demokratische Republik Kongo |
| Denmark | Dänemark |
| Egypt | Ägypten |
| Estonia | Estland |
| Finland | Finnland |
| France | Frankreich |
| Georgia | Georgien |
| Germany | Deutschland |
| Great Britain | Großbritannien |
| Greece | Griechenland |
| Greenland | Grönland |
| Hungary | Ungarn |
| Iran | Der Iran |
| Iraq | Der Irak |
| Italy | Italien |
| Ivory Coast | Die Republik Elfenbeinküste, Die Republik Côte d'Ivoire |

| English | German |
|---|---|
| Latvia | Lettland |
| Lebanon | Der Libanon |
| Lithuania | Litauen |
| Luxembourg | Luxemburg |
| Mexico | Mexiko |
| Moldova | (Republik) Moldau |
| Mongolia | Die Mongolei |
| Morocco | Marokko |
| Netherlands | Die Niederlande |
| New Zealand | Neuseeland |
| Nigeria | Nigeria |
| Norway | Norwegen |
| Oman | Der Oman |
| Poland | Polen |
| Republic of the Congo | Der Kongo |
| Romania | Rumänien |
| Sardinia | Sardinien |
| Sicily | Sizilien |
| Slovakia | Die Slowakei |
| South Africa | Südafrika |
| Spain | Spanien |
| Sudan | Der Sudan |
| Sweden | Schweden |
| Switzerland | Die Schweiz |
| Turkey | Die Türkei |
| Ukraine | Ukraine |
| United Arab Emirates | Die Vereinigten Arabischen Emirate |
| United States | Die Vereinigten Staaten, Die USA |
| Vatican City | Der Vatikan |
| Yemen | Der Jemen |

# BOOKS OF THE BIBLE

## *THE OLD TESTAMENT*

| English | German |
|---|---|
| Genesis | 1. Mose, Genisis |
| Exodus | 2. Mose, Exodus |
| Leviticus | 3. Mose, Levitikus |
| Numbers | 4. Mose, Numeri |
| Deuteronomy | 5. Mose, Deuteronomium |
| Joshua | Josua |
| Judges | Richter |
| Ruth | Rut |
| 1 Samuel | 1. Samuel |
| 2 Samuel | 2. Samuel |
| 1 Kings | 1. Könige |
| 2 Kings | 2. Könige |
| 1 Chronicles | 1. Chronik |
| 2 Chronicles | 2. Chronik |
| Ezra | Esra |
| Nehemiah | Nehemia |
| Esther | Ester |
| Job | Hiob |
| Psalms | Psalmen |
| Proverbs | Sprüche |
| Ecclesiastes | Prediger |
| Song of Solomon | Hohelied |
| Isaiah | Jesaja |
| Jeremiah | Jeremia |
| Lamentations | Klagelieder |
| Ezekiel | Hesekiel |
| Daniel | Daniel |
| Hosea | Hosea |
| Joel | Joel |
| Amos | Amos |
| Obadiah | Obadja |
| Jonah | Jona |
| Micah | Mica |
| Nahum | Nahum |

| English | German |
|---|---|
| Habakkuk | Habakuk |
| Zephaniah | Zephanja |
| Haggai | Haggai |
| Zechariah | Sacharja |
| Malachi | Maleachi |

## *THE NEW TESTAMENT*

| English | German |
|---|---|
| Matthew | Matthäus |
| Mark | Markus |
| Luke | Lukas |
| John | Johannes |
| Acts | Apostelgeschichte |
| Romans | Römer |
| 1 Corinthians | 1. Korinther |
| 2 Corinthians | 2. Korinther |
| Galatians | Galater |
| Ephesians | Epheser |
| Philippians | Philipper |
| Colossians | Kolosser |
| 1 Thessalonians | 1. Thessalonicher |
| 2 Thessalonians | 2. Thessalonicher |
| 1 Timothy | 1. Timotheus |
| 2 Timothy | 2. Timotheus |
| Titus | Titus |
| Philemon | Philemon |
| Hebrews | Hebräer |
| James | Jakobus |
| 1 Peter | 1. Petrus |
| 2 Peter | 2. Petrus |
| 1 John | 1. Johannes |
| 2 John | 2. Johannes |
| 3 John | 3. Johannes |
| Jude | Judas |
| Revelation | Offenbarung |

*THE APOCRYPHA*

| English | German |
|---|---|
| Judith | Judith |
| Wisdom | Weisheit |
| Tobit | Tobit |
| Sirach | Sirach |
| Baruch | Baruch |
| 1 Maccabees | 1. Makkabäer |
| 2 Maccabees | 2. Makkabäer |
| Additions to Esther | Ergänzungen zu Esther |
| Additions to Daniel | Ergänzungen zu Daniel |

## ZODIAC SIGNS

| English | German |
|---|---|
| Aquarius | Der Wassermann, Die Wassermänner |
| Pisces | Die Fische |
| Aries | Der Widder, Die Widder |
| Taurus | Der Stier, Die Stiere |
| Gemini | Der Zwilling, Die Zwillinge |
| Cancer | Der Krebs, Die Krebse |
| Leo | Der Löwe, Die Löwen |
| Virgo | Die Jungfrau, Die Jungfrauen |
| Libra | Die Waage, Die Waagen |
| Scorpio | Der Skorpion, Die Skorpione |
| Sagittarius | Der Schütze, Die Schützen |
| Capricorn | Der Steinbock, Die Steinböcke |

# APPENDIX

# GLOSSARY

## GLOSSARY OF TERMS

| Term | Definition |
|---|---|
| article | word that indicates whether a noun is specific (*the*) or general (*a* or *an*) |
| case | function of a noun in a sentence |
| direct object | object being acted upon by the subject |
| indirect object | object that receives the direct object, or object to or for whom (or which) the subject's action is done |
| noun | person, place, or thing |
| object | noun or pronoun not used as a subject |
| preposition | word that indicates a relationship between the noun or pronoun and another part of the sentence (examples: *for, to, from, on, in, at, with, by*) |
| pronoun | word that substitutes for a noun (examples: *I, me, we, us, you, he, him, she, her, it, they, them*) |
| subject | noun or pronoun that performs the action |
| verb | action that is performed |

## GLOSSARY OF ABBREVIATIONS

| Abbreviation | Term |
|---|---|
| ACC | accusative case |
| DAT | dative case |
| DO | direct object |
| F | feminine (a gender of nouns) |
| GEN | genitive case |
| IO | indirect object |
| M | masculine (a gender of nouns) |
| MFNP | masculine, feminine, neuter, plural |
| N | neuter (a gender of nouns) |
| NOM | nominative case |
| P | plural |
| *zB* | *zum Beispiel (for example)* |

## OTHER REFERENCES

*REVIEW OF KEY RULES*

| Rule | Location in the Text |
|---|---|
| Nouns that are not the subject of a sentence are objects; objects can be either direct or indirect. | Review > Nouns: Subjects and Objects |
| A noun's function in the sentence determines its case. | Review > Cases |
| Generally, word order is Subject + Verb + More Nouns + More Verbs. The king of all rules is this: The verb always comes in the second place. | Review > Basic Word Order |
| A noun's gender and case determine its articles, pronouns, and endings for its adjectives (as well as the noun itself sometimes). | Gender > Declension |
| Direct objects are in the accusative case, and indirect objects are in the dative case. | Case |
| Gender does not affect word order, but case does. | Case > Cases and Word Order |
| When a sentence includes both a direct object and indirect object, the order for noun cases becomes Nominative + Dative + Accusative (NDA). | Case > Cases and Word Order |
| Prepositions clarify case in the word order of time, manner, and place (TMP). | Case > Cases and Word Order |
| The pronoun is closer than any nouns to the verb regardless of the pronoun's gender, number, or case. | Pronouns Before Considering Genitive Case > Pronouns and Word Order |
| When a sentence includes both DO and IO pronouns, the sentence structure changes to Subject (nominative) + Verb + DO (accusative) + IO (dative), with noun and pronoun cases in the order of Nad, where the lowercase letters indicate pronoun cases. | Pronouns Before Considering Genitive Case > Pronouns and Word Order |

| Rule | Location in the Text |
|------|----------------------|
| When there is motion toward an object (i.e., going from one space to another), that noun will be the DO, in the accusative case; otherwise, it will be dative. | Wishy-Washy Prepositions |
| When adjectives come after a noun and verb, they are simple. When an adjective precedes a noun, though, the adjective declines with the article. | Adjectives |

## *REVIEW OF PREPOSITIONS*

| Accusative | Dative | Wishy-Washy | Genitive |
|------------|--------|-------------|----------|
| durch | aus | an | (an)statt |
| für | außer | auf | außerhalb |
| gegen | bei | hinter | beiderseits |
| ohne | mit | in | diesseits |
| um | nach | neben | infolge |
| bis | seit | über | innerhalb |
| | von | unter | mithilfe |
| | zu | vor | trotz |
| | (others) | zwischen | um … willen |
| | | | während |
| | | | wegen |
| | | | (others) |

# ABOUT THE AUTHOR

C.S. Stahlman was born in 1958 during his father's senior year at the University of Illinois.

As an exchange student in 1976, he lived with Familie Drechsler near Kulmbach (Oberfranken), and he stays in touch with them, mostly with their daughter, Margit. Kulmbach is where he met the future mother of his son, Matthew.

Graduating in 1980 from Westminster College in Missouri with a BA in history, and commissioned into the US Army, he served as liaison officer to the III German Korps for the 97th Signal Battalion. Living "on the economy," he made friends among the residents of Viernheim and Biblis in what was then West Germany. Biblis is where he married his first wife in 1983.

In 2010 he returned to Oberfranken after discovering the Stahlman family was from the region (known as Hummelgau). There he stayed with and got to know Familie Nützel, distant relatives. He stays in contact with Carola, who contributed to this book with her understanding of some confusing nuances of meaning, and her husband, Georg Nützel. They and their Tante Renate and Onkel Siegfried took Mr. Stahlman to the church to see the baptismal font where his great-great-grandparents were baptized in the 1830s. None of this would have happened without his interest in German, and that motivates him to encourage foreign language study, knowing its benefits are not limited to just words and rules.

www.ingramcontent.com/pod-product-compliance
Lightning Source LLC
Chambersburg PA
CBHW070922130626
46555CB00001B/250